Kissing the Bread

Acts of Attention: The Poems of D. H. Lawrence

In the Fourth World: Poems

The Summer Kitchen: Poems

Emily's Bread: Poems

Blood Pressure: Poems

Wrongful Death: A Memoir

Ghost Volcano: Poems

*The Madwoman in the Attic:
The Woman Writer and the 19th Century Literary Imagination*
(with Susan Gubar)

*No Man's Land:
The Place of the Woman Writer in the 20th Century*
(in three volumes, with Susan Gubar)

Masterpiece Theatre: An Academic Melodrama
(with Susan Gubar)

Shakespeare's Sisters: Feminist Essays on Women Poets
(editor, with Susan Gubar)

The Norton Anthology of Literature by Women: The Tradition in English
(editor, with Susan Gubar)

The House Is Made of Poetry: Essays on the Art of Ruth Stone
(editor, with Wendy Barker)

MotherSongs: Poems For, By, and About Mothers
(editor, with Susan Gubar and Diana O'Hehir)

Kissing the Bread

New & Selected Poems, 1 9 6 9 – 1 9 9 9

by Sandra M. Gilbert

W. W. NORTON & COMPANY
NEW YORK / LONDON

For information about permission to reproduce selections from this book, write to
Permissions, W. W. Norton & Company, Inc., 500 Fifth Avenue,
New York, NY 10110

The text of this book is composed in Weiss with the display set in Weiss
Composition by Gina Webster
Manufacturing by Courier Westford
Book design by BTDnyc

LIBRARY OF CONGRESS CATALOGING-IN-PUBLICATION DATA

Gilbert, Sandra M.
Kissing the bread : new & selected poems, 1969–1999 / by Sandra M. Gilbert.
p.   cm.
ISBN 0-393-04941-8
I. Title.
PS3557.I34227 K57 2000
811'.54—dc21

00-027764

W. W. Norton & Company, Inc., 500 Fifth Avenue, New York, N.Y. 10110
www.wwnorton.com

W. W. Norton & Company Ltd., 10 Coptic Street, London WC1A 1PU
1 2 3 4 5 6 7 8 9 0

For my mother,
ANGELA CARUSO MORTOLA,
who helped poetry happen

Contents

II. Want

III. When She Was Kissed by the Mathematician

IV. At Cleopatra Bay

VII. From *Emily's Bread* (1984)

VIII. *The Summer Kitchen* (1983)

IX. From *In the Fourth World* (1979)

Acknowledgments

American Poetry Review: "Journal Entry, 1984," "The Language of Flowers"

Beloit Poetry Journal: "The Mall," "Going to Connecticut," "Thirty Years Later I Meet Your Seventeen-Year-Old Daughter the Poet"

Field: "Spoon," "Dark Blue," "Trunk," "Calvados"

Michigan Quarterly Review: "Trionfo del Morte"

Ontario Review: "The Outsider," "The Hypothetical Life," "The Tidal Wave," "Last Sunday at *Les Grands Eaux Musicales*"

Open Places: "After Long Rain,"

Ploughshares: "God, He Had a Hat!" "Walking the Seawall,"

Poetry: "The Magi in Florida, 1988," "About the Beginning," "Seizure," "Indoor Camellia," "Mother-in-Law," "In the Garage of the Retirement Complex," "Gold Tooth," "Against Poetry," "The Mountains," "Memory Fails," "October Cobwebs," "Basil," "Fog on the Coast," "Enormous Wind," "November Afternoon," "Autumn, Como"

Solo: "After the Freeze," "Aurora Borealis"

Sycamore Review: "Epithalamion"

TriQuarterly: "Death," "Want," "Omens," "At Cleopatra Bay," "Shelling Beans Outside Pollenca," "Catedral at Tlacolula," "Hurtigruten"

VIA: "Uncle Barney"

A Note to the Reader

Some of the new poems in this collection—notably, a number of the pieces in Section I, "The Magi in Florida"—actually predate the poems gathered in *Ghost Volcano* (1995), a volume of elegies for my husband, Elliot Gilbert, that disrupted all the writing I was doing at the time of his unexpected death in 1991. Now, after slowly, painfully, resuming (and of course in many ways changing) work on earlier material, I have tried to assimilate poems from the late eighties and early nineties into the body of verse that began to unfold for me after I completed *Ghost Volcano.*

As always, I'm grateful to many colleagues for advice and inspiration, among them members of my poetry group in Berkeley—Diana O'Hehir, Alan Williamson, Chana Bloch, Peter Dale Scott, Phyllis Stowell, and Jeanne Foster—along with my companion David Gale, my three children Roger, Kathy, and Susanna Gilbert—and my dear friend the late Bob Griffin.

—SANDRA M. GILBERT
Berkeley/Paris 1999

I

The Magi in Florida

The Magi in Florida, 1988

November. The sun is tethered in its southern arc,
and this, he says, is the season when
the magi come, the ones who are

the ministers of middle age, late year,
the ones with gifts more strange than myrrh,
more absolute than frankincense.

We lie on the beach at the out-of-date resort,
cradled in damp sand, oiled and waiting.
Flashes of heat, then clots of cloud

stripe the toppling waves.
Are the wise travelers gathering now in the west,
in the swamps of the Everglades,

on slippery banks where marsh hens brood?
Are they cramming some words for us
into their heavy sacks?

He says, *while we still can,*
while we're young enough—
But as the sun dips

into the tropics, trailing a halo
of scarlet impossibles, we feel
the three old ones draw nearer:

they ride on the backs of cryptic
beasts, they follow a star
we can't quite see,

and they move
in a grave caravan
out of the tall sword grass

toward the brief hard strip of land
where both of us are stranded, wondering,
without angels, without manger,

without family.

About the Beginning

The nastiness of origins!
when she put on that pink shantung,

she wasn't thinking of you;
straightening his tie, he was equally

indifferent. Their blind date
with your destiny was just another

dumb night out. At the restaurant,
his best friend joked that the wine

was "unpretentious" while hers
kept visiting the ladies room

to change her Kotex. The Italian waiter
scowled and limped but didn't

belong to the Mafia. Nobody
drank too much, nobody

told any interesting stories. He
thought maybe he'd see her once or twice again.

She thought he was too skinny, she was
really stuck on a flashy

lawyer in Brooklyn and this shy
guy just had a dull job with the city.

As for you, you didn't know the difference
between yourself and any other egg.

No, you were only half a cell, stranded among
slick membranes, and when

they had married and copulated and you'd swelled
alarmingly into a body

with fingerprints intact
and you were inching out of *her* body

in short sharp jerks,
she was only thinking about the awful

pain this whole business was causing her
because she still didn't know who you were—

you with your booties and your allergies,
your sonnets and your discoveries:

you were still lighter in her thought
than the silk flower on the straw hat

she'd planned to wear on that fatal date
and then forgotten about.

The Dolls

hid in the toy box,
stuffed with the mysterious kapok
that she said was making me sick:

Heidi, round-faced, kinky haired;
Clara, her giant ragged friend;
daddy's Genovese sailor lad;

and those odd pals, the bride
and Carmen Miranda
and the black-masked carnival panda. . . .

All banished to the foyer closet,
secreted with lock and key
from friends and "crooks" and me!

"A rag and a clothespin," she said,
"should be enough for any kid."
And she should know, she added,

mother and teacher for all those years!
The blue walls of the bedroom shed no tears,
the rabbit knitted into the tattered rug was silent

the way the little girl was silent when she went
into the witch's house
and understood she was as tiny as a mouse

and the witch knew exactly what to do
with the heavy key to the oven and the torn-up
bodies meant for the Sunday stew.

The little girl was silent and sad and sorry
that the dolls were going so far away,
and only the dolls refused to worry

because they were sure how they meant to live in the closet,
they knew they'd never forget
the glittering Alps that had long ago glazed their button eyes,

the oranges that winked on magic islands,
the swaggering Mediterranean on which they once had gazed,
the midnight bedroom's gates of ivory and horn,

and O yes, the door inside the blue wall, the secret door
that might at any minute open
onto the terrible tundra

where their fur was born.

Uncle Barney

Half a century in the madhouse: how
did the seasons go?
You were a boy when they put you there—
"brilliant" and frantic.

You "thought" you were "a girl," my mother said.
She was fifteen. Sicilian.
Had to interpret your craziness
for American doctors.

Brooklyn lowered its gray stone guts
over your head.
You got on the subway.
City College would help. And Virgil.

Uncle Joe the pharmacist chanted Virgil.
You were nineteen. The windows quivered.
Flashing membranes.
What was on the other side?

"He put his fist through the pane," my mother said.
She wanted to think you were dead.
Outside the high glass of the Long Island sick house
leaves fell and swelled and fell.

Crumbling orange, popping green.
Colors bursting over and over
like glass slowly shattering,
then faster, faster.

Probably the television was on
for the last quarter of a century.
You started with *Ozzie and Harriet*.
Then *Star Trek*. Spock.

Leaves flamed and bubbled,
shades of Palermo, where you were nine
when Uncle Joe shouted defiance in the piazza
and the family had to flee.

White corridors unwound.
Your old notebooks were gone.
You loved a nurse named—what?—
who sometimes helped you pee.

Your bathrobe fell open.
Your knees ached.
The screen glimmered like a window.
Wars and soap operas. Jello.

When I was fifteen my mother told me about you.
In cosy Queens, I read your notebooks.
The El still rampaged past the Williamsburg brownstone
you once lived in,

shattering windows, dusting tomato plants.
I was watching *I Love Lucy*
amid bricks and windows.
I hope you loved Lucy too.

I hope you chatted in Sicilian with Sulu.
I hope when your bathrobe opened
the nighttime birds of Palermo
rose from the folds of your body

shrieking a Latin no one else
will ever know.

Going to Connecticut

—for J.R.

More than a third of a century later,
meeting for the first time in almost all those years,

we face each other's still somewhat familiar faces
across a table in a California restaurant,

and wonder why we did it, why we suddenly said
that night in July in Greenwich Village

"Let's go to Connecticut," and got on a train
and ended up at midnight in Old Greenwich, Connecticut,

holding hands on an empty road that wound past
serious grown-up sleeping houses. . . .

Well, I was fifteen, you were nearly twenty-one, we were
    experimentally
"in love," and I guess it must have seemed

like "something to do"—better than Remo anyway,
or the coffee houses, or the Eighth Street Bookstore,

even, in that scratchy heat,
better than Jones Beach: the long low

sober train boring into a wall of black, the alien
townships spurting past on either side

(nothing very built up then),
each with its deserted, brilliant platform

waiting for the next day's passengers, the real
people who really needed to ride that train.

How cindery the windows were,
and spooky with moths outside the glamorous

club car where we sat with sodas
on itchy plush reclining seats!

And how the crickets simmered
where we got out, dizzy on 7UP!

Remember the hedges—lilac, honeysuckle—
along the way, as we walked toward

we didn't know where?
                    We kissed a little

under one, tasting salt and 7UP
on each other, not sure what next

or where, then peered at
the shadows on lawn after lawn, the dim

bulk of chimneys, shapes of shutters,
here a trike, there a plastic pool,

and couples snoring, mysterious,
behind those tall white walls,

until we got embarrassed, still not sure what next,
retraced our steps, boarded another train,

and were hurried back to where we came from,
feeling like voyeurs, like trespassers.

Thirty Years Later I Meet Your
Seventeen-Year-Old Daughter the Poet

—in memory of R.I.S.

1.
Would I know her anywhere, this child
who never knew *you* except in photographs?

She has your high clear polished forehead, but
"No, my sister has his dimple, the cleft
in his chin . . ."
                    Tight curly hair (like yours)
drawn back, and your face, thinned, refined,
to a girl's—you in a girl's body, you
(thick, muscular, tempestuous)
newly slight, polite: *you* in a neat
print skirt, loose black blouse!

Now a seventeen-year-old classicist—
"Latin's my favorite"—you translate
Catullus, write tidy sonnets, envy the sister
who remembers the dead father,
but (as you always did) adore your mother
and walk with your head thrown slightly back
as if the weight of thought were hard to bear.

I rock in my teacherly chair.
She's shy, constrained.
"I don't want to read my father's poems,
they're all in tatters in the closet,
they scare me."

I tell her
I'm a kind of long-lost aunt, tell her
about the photo of you as (you said) "the young Shelley"—
about your huntsman's bow, opera, baseball,
endless games of chess in the dorm parlor with you
boasting your prowess.

                    And she's embarrassed,
you're embarrassed, living in her blood,
to think you ever acted like that!

2.

When you were a man, a thirty-seven-year-old,
long after our last fight, last kiss,
you OD'd on morphine
and disappeared into the blanks
that always framed your mind.

But she's sent two poems and a thank-you note,
and her handwriting—yours—hasn't changed.
"It meant a lot to me to talk about my dad,"
you scribbled with your new small fingers.

I want to believe this, want to believe
you're really starting out again!

Do me a favor:
                forget
Catullus, Horace, love and hate
and think, instead, of the epic
cell, the place where the chromosomes
are made and made for a moment perfect.

Translate those lines from Virgil
some of us once liked to chant,
the ones about beginning, about those who first
left Troy to seek the Italian shore.

The Mall

Let me tell you about the mall. Right now
no one's screaming in the middle of the mall,
no one's trying to kill herself,
no one's fists are showing.

Above the mall, there's a great tipped-over goblet of air through
    which we all move
like motes of dust, but more purposeful,
as the steep calm escalators glide up and down,
oblivious of us.

Along the wide tiled corridors of the mall,
there are benches and potted palms, where young mothers
smoke and gossip, rocking strollers, and old impatient men
wait for their wives to buy "housewares."

Sometimes small bands play where two vast passages meet.
Sometimes people with bells and boxes ask for coins.
Along this wall, you'll find beads and rings.
Along that one, robes, soaps, spices.

From nine A.M. till midnight you hear a scuff and sidle
wearing away the floor. From midnight till nine,
you hear the slide of mops, the sigh of escalators,
the hiss as air-conditioning changes tempo.

Believe me, this poem isn't going to be ironic about the mall,
this poem remembers the *souk* and the *marketplatz*,
the bonfires that lit the settlement in Idaho.
This poem promises to think about daffodils and spotted owls
    tomorrow.

Right now this particular poem is pouring its Beaujolais
all over the shuffling yawning mall,
where the salesgirls are just locking up their cash registers,
where the cleaning people are wheeling out their heavy carts,

where the fluorescent streetlights are buzzing
above the mostly empty parking lot
and the decorative red cabbages in concrete planters
are closing, closing into their own still cores.

Seizure

Invisible fists fling you from the bed,
pummel you, quake through your body,
hammer you toward another place, another shape,
an island where a high wind

cries all night in black branches
and you're a bird lost in the storm,
without a voice, without a name,
without parents.

I stand by, two thousand miles away,
wringing my hands,
mother of pain, mother
of sorrow, remembering

how they strapped my feet into the stirrups,
how they fastened my wrists with leather cuffs,
how they clamped the gas mask over my face,
how invisible fists pounded my belly,

how I shrieked with love
as I gave you up to this tempest-
blasted island of wind
from which I can't save you,

though I'd grieve and slave
to have you back in the calm center
of the storm, the miraculous island
where I'm always your mother.

The Outsider

I haunt the edges of your life:
through the fringes of the fancy shade,
through the beaded curtain,

I see you frowning at your desk, I see you
in your yellow kitchen, feel the heat
that rises from the oven where

your bread is swelling, see you
naked, spreading the quilt
on your marriage bed,

and yes, you know
I'm there, you know
when your children dance by the fire after dinner

I pulse in their steps, they leap
to my beat, and when
you slam the book down on the desk

I am the one who slams it down, who
pushes it away, who tells you
to burn it up,

and when, late at night,
ice cracks the panes of your study window
and you rise, tiptoe to the front door, draw it slowly

open and stand alone on the stoop
in January cold
watching the cars go by on the long street,

I am what you see in the flaring lights,
what you hear, shivering,
in the black speed of the tires.

Broth

Its steam.
The bones and carrots of it.

They say, "A broth of a boy."
They mean, *Erotic broth.*

Hearts of celery,
heart of *you.*

I pour and stir, skim,
strain, purify.

The stove's alive with muttering
flames and whispers.

Your hand clasps mine,
lips open.

Salt and sweet,
the broth embraces itself:

it's fat and gold,
the color of large fields in the far west.

Expansive and hot and stupid,
it's what we tell ourselves we want.

Indoor Camellia

How absurd you are—in the fake spring
of a November greenhouse edging
an east coast living room—
to keep on blossoming!

Parched leaves layer the lawn
just beyond your branches, and on
the dying elm a last thin few fling
supplicant colors up and down.

Naive, the pinkish-red of rare roast beef,
your ruffled petals preen and droop, as if
hoping against hope for tropic damp,
for heat, heat, four-season heat,

and lovers, oiled bodies, balms
of darkness, sleepy streams:
although you may be dumb, you aren't
shy, you flaunt your charms!

I brood on the sofa with my drink,
wondering at such temerity, such frank-
ness about sex. You stunted fool,
your flowers seem to think

love can happen anywhere, or any
time—
    and yet your black-green bony
leaves say *no*, say *don't let go,*

say *hang on to the salts of the earth,*
forget the honey.

Journal Entry, 1984

Almost February, plums just stalled in bud,
football Sunday, only women and babies on the streets,
and I drive around town thinking of
what I wanted, how I framed the chain
of months and rains and flowers
in a calendar of my desire,

wanting to be wanted,
wanting to want, sentimental
as some nineteenth-century heroine who crowns herself with
    pink
imaginary petals—O how
I dreamed my days away, an invalid on
window seats, a lover between sheets of fever,

and now from the still center
where gifts are given
come daily packages of ice,
and I wonder, blue in the supermarket parking lot,
if this failure of the calendar, this refusal of blossoms
is middle age. . . .

                    Sunset.
The chill trees darken and sharpen
their edges, the cold cups of the magnolia
shred in a small wind: it's really
winter still, beyond
the scrim of spring.

Who were you, that I wanted so?

Husbands and fathers hunch behind flickering windows
in closed houses, women push strollers
pointlessly along clear streets,
and I try to remember, as I drive away,
where I set out to get to,
why I'm not yet there.

Mother-in-Law

The title sags. Old flesh, too weak
to stand alone. Hyphens

help us along, contrive the bleak chatter
of pseudo-mother and not-quite-daughter

stuck on some interminable
out-of-season cruise.

No one offers
broth or shuffleboard, we're

left to our own polite
devices, searching your fancy coffee table

for new topics, pretending neither
notices the sluggish foot, the stink

of grown-up grown-old diapers.
Your son tells jokes, mine

escorts his wife from the room.
In another hour this visit will be done

and we'll drape you over the squat
chair in the corner

like a tatty chenille bathrobe
someone's sooner or later

going to tell me I have to put on.

In the Garage of the Retirement Complex

I've never seen so many clean
white cars: the south coast salt
must scour them!
Ranged in rows like incubators,

they shine in the dusk that rises
from the tropical golf course,
a sort of laudanum haze, and I
brood beside the out-of-place red Ford

my husband rented yesterday
while he wheels his mother upstairs
for a pee.
                Another blur of slick

dove-white, and in comes a long low
Cadillac with somebody else's
husband, somebody else's hunched up
mother-in-law. . . .

                And then
the oldest ones arrive, clinging
together out of nothing more
than need—the bald bland geezer

with his mouth ajar, and his
shrunken, smiling, spotted wife,
greeting me, greeting *me*,
indistinct in the twilight,

as the steady chair comes rolling back,
ready for the restaurant,
cradling a dead weight
in a chalk-white pantsuit.

Gold Tooth

Mouth agape, you twist in
the hands of the dentist.
Outside, what the poet called "midwinter spring"
trails its eagerness across the trees,

plum blossoms foaming up in a hurry,
camellias bursting open as if to whisper
Quick! Quick!
while the dentist pokes, scrapes, polishes.

He's making you a gold tooth,
"mouth jewelry," he jokes;
he's making you a tooth
that will glow like no other;

month by month he's replacing your frailty
with precious metals.
You think you love your softness, your
pink, your lips that smile, purse, murmur,

you think you love
your tongue, that sweet camellia petal,
but the dentist has made a plaster
model of your bite:

pale artifact, it sits on his counter,
tough as a Neolithic axe, your fat
gold tooth wedged into one tight crevice.
The dentist knows this bite is what counts,

this bite, and this immortal tooth.
His back to the blossoming window,
he sends a rush of cold along your gums,
then taps your new treasure

into your new wound
with a tiny mallet that tells you
only what is hard enough to endure
will endure.

God, He Had a Hat!

Mrs. Rabinowitz is sitting on the beach with her little grandson, who is playing in the sand with a pail and shovel when a great tidal wave suddenly appears and sweeps him out to sea.

Mrs. Rabinowitz (shaking her fist at the sky): God, bring him back! Bring that little boy right back!

Another tidal wave appears and deposits the grandson on the beach, next to Mrs. Rabinowitz.

Mrs. Rabinowitz (after scrutinizing the child for a minute):
God, he had a hat!

It's the fifties and we stand in the doorway kissing,
suited in the decorum of our age,
shameless in ignorance.

Our betrothal kisses are small, soft,
nervous as rabbits venturing toward the yard
where the mastiff lunges on his chain and the chain

rattles its gravity across concrete.
But my nineteen-year-old
stance is gracious and wifely,

as if bidding an office-bound spouse goodbye,
although I feel the weird prod of your hard-on
poking against gray wool.

Goodbye, goodbye, sweetheart!
Goodbye to your graduate-student face,
your face of a young cynic that blurs as I kiss it!

Goodbye to your innocent almost-pompadour
(soon to be shaved in Basic by the 4th AD)!
Goodbye to the startled fur of your brows!

Past midnight, we're through kissing, my father
waits in his fat chair, his haze of smoke,
and you dissolve into the vague hall,

the leafy sidewalks, the lit-up all-night
subways whose overheated cars
rumble into the dark like stage sets.

But now your hat swims back to me,
the one you're wearing in the snapshot
just outside the honeymoon hotel—

gray felt, prematurely middle-aged,
with a brim stiff as cardboard and a crown
that was kind and crushable and soft,

soft as a peach to the touch. . . .

Variations on a Theme*

Ghosts: Glenn Gould singing, the track
of the voice of the dead man
tunelessly intoning, a ghost

cantata behind the ghost
of the Goldbergs on a compact
disk I can carry in the deepest

pocket of my winter coat,
and that uncontrollable
bass breaking in

and in on Bach . . .
and the sudden living glint
of my dead father's eyes

in the photo someone
took when he was twenty-one,
a blade-faced boy

whose shining gaze
still follows me around the room,
the Goldbergs pacing in the background:

maybe when we come in from the zero
air we bring these
shadows in our pockets, they're

*Despite the best efforts of technicians, Glenn Gould's humming could never
be erased from the masters.

folded into silence,
dim electrons leaking
from the speakers.

Some nights we wake up sweating:
the picture's out of the frame, the voice
escaped from the soundproof studio

in a thin cadenza
that crawls like smoke
under the edge of the bedroom door,

humming, crooning:
I want you to hear me,
I want to see you.

I am the theme.
Everything else
is only a variation.

After the Freeze

Forget about myths and seasons!
Flat January, timid daylight, early dark.
The long blank field, severe with crows, leans westward,
huddling toward a sorry sun,
and one black pickup traces the horizon.

Last week lemons froze in the valley.
On my deck, geraniums wilted like old lettuce.
Now tule fog, weak as my own
imagination of the spirit world,
unfurls a skeptic's stage-set for resurrection.

As if Orpheus knew what he might find down there
under the rotting compost! As if his sweet
Eurydice glowed in the dark, a bulb
that would really flower again!
—And you, you stupid crows,

what seeds do you find in the crumbling furrow?
Today the tall chill sky
says no, the puckered skin of the lemon,
preaching finality,
says Eurydice is really dead.

The Scar

tells its story daily, tracing
a mean lean before-and-after
on my hand. Fat

of the flesh lapses away,
skin flakes and frizzles, nerves
flick little flames against

the surgeon's almost microscopic
needle holes. Hour
by hour the scar

emerges, scarlet
signal, track of the past.
I'm glad it's there, I

stroke it, cozen it: it tells me
about smashed glass, about bloody
bathtubs, about all the bad

in being that might make
being good. Some nights,
as I fall asleep,

I imagine it's a skinny
road I ride,
dragging the slack

wagon of my moods
as if I were provisioning
a failing army.

Like history,
this road will always be there.
Like history,

it'll tighten and fade
and tighten and slowly
sink into the ruts of my body.

October 31, 1995: A Ghost in Goldwin Smith

In honorem
Goldwini Smith.
—MCMVI

Rollerblades
ARE NOT
Allowed
In
This Building.

It's almost a year since I wrote a poem where
I used the word (not just a letter) *I*.
As in, *I saw, I thought, I felt*, or even
He and I. As in, *I was. Was here.*

And maybe a ghost would be this shy,
this tenuous. Maybe Halloween,
with its scary hilarity's about
recursions of that single arrogant pronoun,

vulgarly pronouncing itself
in the dark where it should just
shut up, stop staking
its dreary claims.

But *I*, yes *I* am the ghost who was just called forth.
I am the one in the hooded jacket, the Paris scarf,
who passes not quite silently enough
into the classroom building of forty years ago,

the one who slides not quite unseen
—in fact, conspicuous in the leathery
glaze of middle age—along the hardly
different corridors, the one who whispers

I and *I thought,* and *I felt,* and *he and I*
around the corner from the Coke machine
that wasn't there *when he and I* so must be
less substantial than the breathless girl

who once had *me* and *I* for every
step of the Via Dolorosa of this hall.
Where today my favorite professor
faces me across his desk,

quite unabashed by ghosts like me.
He after all has taught
my dying generation with the others
who have trod, have trod.

And tread in their with-it
jeans the soggy quad
where keen damp winds swirl all the spectral
pronouns past the classroom windows.

He says he's moving to a ritzy "home"
with indoor swimming, nursing.
Says his wife still hates the thought
but "just for now" she's "going along . . ."

"Forty years," wrote my once best friend
in last week's e-mail.
You and I, you and I,
our whispers drift the old warm halls

in ceremonial day-of-the-dead attire.
Nor is the "structure" certain what to do:
it greets with anxious babble—
in honorem . . . Rollerblades. . . .

But still the *I*'s have it, murmuring
their insistence on who he, what she,
when I and they. . . .
Even after I leave

the stony barrack of the past,
the diffident new autumn trees
agree it's never too late to mourn, never
too late to rollerblade along the edges

of my own enduring ignorance—
the innocence that was just confusion,
the wisdom that was only
a stuttering will to the life of *I* and *I*.

Berkeley, February 11, 1998:
The Hypothetical Life

After a week of rain, the sky
shedding its thousand mystery
meanings, a flood of sun

drenches the garden,
lights up the twigs the branches
of the hypothetical life—

the life that escaped the surgeon's scalpel,
the blood that rained
from tubes they planted in you.

No wind today. The rhododendrons
barely beckon: but O how the saw-toothed
leaves of the great oaks

glow in the massive stillness of that life
through which we've walked caressed
and quarreled all these seven years,

still man and wife and wife
and man—*und Weib und Mann*—like
Papageno/Papagena still

alive *durch die Lieb' allein,*
still feathered
with pleasure and the delicate matching

plumages of marriage.
Though on the real white real-life
wall where your likeness

hangs in an artist's pencilled
effigy the curves of arm and jaw
begin to fade, the fine

details of beard to blur, as if
the sky and its surly
mists had started

leaking through the graphite
outline, leaving only
the hypothetical

person that you were,
cracking cryptic
jokes in the wavering

mind of the rainy garden.

Ending the Book

The problem is always ending the book.
The premises of opening are easy:
pages unfold like chromosomes,
each shred of meaning needing the next.
In the great space of beginning,
everything makes sense.
The Topics—Love, Death, Art, Desire—
branch out inexorable,
veins through which the blood of thought
drags phrases to the heart.

But as you shuffle paper, voices
nibble at the edge of clarity.
Your mother, plaintive: "Why
must you be so morbid, you were
such a happy child!" Your friends:
"This doesn't *sound* like you."
Your editor: "That doesn't seem to fit."
Something's been left over, out.
Should you throw it all together
in a final part, an odd miscellany?

You sweat at dawn.
The space is empty now, the choices—
upbeat? elegiac? mean? sincere?—
multiply malignantly.
You've forgotten the plan you anyway
just thought you had.
Is the last word
the only one that counts?
In your dreams you walk backward.
Your outline blurs and disappears.

The Tidal Wave

that toppled me
when I was three
was no doubt only

three feet high
but like a white and spiky
ancestor

it hovered over me
a minute as if brooding
What to do with this one?

then struck, then plunged
upon me—pail and all—
and although through

its hissing veil
of blue-green salt
I saw my parents running,

heard, loud and absurd,
their voices calling
Sandra, Sandra,

the muscles of the tide
held me tight,
dragged me up the shore

over rocks, shells, broken glass,
along the beach
to this high seaweedy place

where—schools and inches,
salt and scars and children—
later, I lie by myself,

years out of their reach.

Walking the Seawall,

pacing the ancient earthworks, the fortifications of silence,
I know I am not through with you, I will never be through,
and not one of us who leap from stone

to stone on the road of boulders
that leads to the old lighthouse, not one of us
who clamber the grassy slope

to the lookout point, not one of us
who tread the path along the shore
next to the tangled wall of morning glory,

not one is through or will ever be through
with your ways of hovering, your
ash in the air, your clouds at daybreak

trailing departure, your echoes of rhyme and joke,
hugs of archaic fleece, smiles
a rubble around us, arms

now sunken, irretrievable. . . .
In your unending
absence we keep on keeping

brave and starched.
Beside the point,
a field of muck sinks into itself:

here we scramble on
splintery boards.
Stench of skunk,

stench of animal grief!
You who were here too, you who waded
in mud beside us,

stand up again in your plaid and freckles
the way you used to once!
Unfurl your striped umbrellas!

Step heavily or lightly, as you did,
twitching and rustling your coats, your furs,
across the bridge from sleep!

Just this single extra
minute
we'll stumble down the uneven beach,

pick our way across the lumps of granite
flung down at water's edge,
creep together just once more

along the jetty at land's end, where
each glittering boulder keeps its fist of stillness
clenched against the wind.

II

Want

Noun:

defect deficiency demerit fault flaw imperfection inadequacy
lack need shortcoming

poverty destitution deficiency deprivation inadequacy indigence lack need privation scarcity

deficit lack dearth deficiency drought famine rarity scarcity
shortage sparseness undersupply

Verb:

require demand expect levy wish

desire crave choose covet envy fancy lust wish

crave ache covet desire hanker hunger itch long lust need
pine thirst yearn

Death

When the great sea turtle came,
dragging its *casita*
of black and white geometry,

and staggered onto the beach
at Puerto Pollenca, its almost phantom
flippers, fin-thin, flailing

faintly as if to ward off
just the old green
buffetings under whose sway

it had swelled from egg
to lizard length, archaic eye
and carapace,

and humped its pain
up the hill of glare and scratch
toward children digging the coarseness up

and the oiled breasts
of mothers and smoking
fathers telling jokes,

and quivered a minute
in its far place,
resting its sorrow a minute,

though the bathers gaped
it had come to die,
nothing inside the hardness

wanted to move, nothing
wanted another drop
of Mediterranean soup,

of flesh or brine
or the pulsing that flickers
among weed and rock,

but the swimmers flung it back
and back into the long deep
life it hated now,

until it drifted, staggered, clambered
onto a hot blank foreign
solid again,

forlorn in its distance,
and the beach boys scooped it
into an iron shovel

and wound it in a trash bag
and bore it off
on a bier of stacked sunbeds,

marching one at the head,
one at the foot,
in the ancient way,

with a trickle of children following,
some shaken and sad, like mourners,
some grinning, even jeering,

as if they were skeptics
(though skeptics about what?)
or scoffers

(but why?).

Code Blue, ICU, Bed 5

1.
The voice on the loudspeaker
—*Code Blue, Code Blue*—

is impassive, a voice
in Grand Central,

announcing
arrivals, departures,

arrivals, departures,
but they run like runners

anyway,
nurses, orderlies,

trundling emergency
into its place,

a space on Bed 5,
a long white platform

where the shadow
of a tall engine

falls as a silent
train draws near,

and a smaller platform, a country station, say,
hidden between thickets, cutbanks,

overgrown with weeds, buzzing with summer,
from which a tiny train,

a local,
is pulling away.

2.

It's summer in the night the small
train enters,
summer, spring, any season

when perfumes make the body ache
and the longing for travel rises,
a cry in the throat.

The nurses and surgeons work like hearts,
their efficient beating
against chest, ribs, lips,

a sound of pistons, a sound
of metal falling on the tracks
again, again,

an engine uselessly following
the local that goes its own way
into a distance ruled

by a blue cryptography:
blue tracks
that keep the train in place,

graphing its journey.

Talk Show

The great lights shatter the ceiling
with their insolence, their nerveless stare.

People turn eager torsos toward the fat white
loops of heat those floodlights shed,

grin, bathe, lave themselves
in the dazzle that laps the stage.

And I too, darling, I too thrust my head and arms
into the glaze of fame: I too come forth

with the crippled, the stained, the scalded by death,
the newly disfigured, the wrecked and the wretched

to blink into the tiny sly unwinking
lenses that range the room.

Ten minutes ago we drifted in the wings,
past the caterer's debris—half-eaten sandwiches,

salads sinking into oil, sticky
nibbles of pastry, unconsoling.

Now, out here in a globe of silence,
we five face the cheer of the hostess,

her glamor, her *sang-froid*, and the quick
flicks of her tense attendants—

ten seconds—NOW—cut—
and urgent, gleaming, we strip to our scars,

while less than the length of a man from us
the audience heaves in its seats,

waves, whispers, pokes at the bars
of its cave of shadow.

Against Poetry

Suddenly I too see
why everybody hates it—
the manifestos of metaphor, the mad
voice that mumbles all night
in the dark: *this is like that, that
is this*, the phosphorescent
flares of vision, the busyness
of words sweeping up
after all that sputter. . . .

When the princess spoke toads
everybody loathed her,
but when her mouth spouted jewels
it was hardly better:

*Not much difference, muttered the courtiers,
between a slide of slime, of jumpy
lumps on the table,
and a spurt of little glittering pellets
hitting you in the eye!*

*It would be better all around
if that lady kept her shapely
lips
tightened on nothing.*

Want

1. Kilninian Kirkyard

Up on the moor what's empty
speaks beyond the speech

(whatever *speech* might mean)
of sheep and birds, speaks

with voices outside the long
long-suffering bleats, the hectic

twittering, and tongues of air
that lick the gravestones clean.

Against the ontology of bracken,
ground bass of hissing thistles,

how absurd the murmurings
of sunstruck wind, its weary natural

history that coils like an adder here
and there above the bog!

And now the sheep set up
their old hilarious clamor

for food and sex and maybe
even eternal life.

2. The Dead

The enormity of them, their
endless arrogance:

the granddad who won't smile
except in dreams, the husband

eternally enraged, the pretty
aunt whose last grimace

is carved in stone,
the newborn bound in a curve of need. . . .

Pour your libations, humble ones
in the sun, pour blood or wine—

and the dead still smile their clever
semblances, false love

in frescoes, photos, friezes—
while their glassy eyes askance

say *no*, say *want*,
say tall in their caves, they want

every cell that never was theirs.

Pour or pray:

the long blank granite family
turns away, dines in the silence

that grips the sullen
spine of the night sky.

3. *I Am*

at the kind west edge
of Mull, green inner island
where a blue flat glimmering
palm of the Atlantic

opens as if in
supplication, as if
begging the land for what
only land can have—

an end to motion, a silencing
of all those dizzy
whispers back and forth
across the shingle.

Grapes on the beach.
And thoughts of the dead
while the summer trippers flail
their kites and sails.

                    I am.
In a hollow of sun among
the dunes. Behind me
a swath of bitten turf.

Am. Without
so many who
opened their sleeves
to the salt the sea

flung toward them once
in hollows of sun
below the high blue
shuddering air. Am.

In the western isles,
July, the sun still high
and the tide rising.
"D'you like the temp.?"

asked the walker I met just now
at damp sand's edge.
 "The air's so cold
the water's warm," I said.

"But it's really cold," he said.
"Cold and it comes fast.
Ten meters in half an hour.
Very cold. Very fast."

The Mountains

It is as if their great silence
has to be watched, as if someone,
it hardly matters which of us,

has to sit for hours on a cold stone
on the cliff that overhangs their green-black lake
and stare as the jagged flanks of ice

let fall their useless mysteries
and stand unveiled, indifferent,
glittering with the force of what they are.

As if we have to stare and stare
for hours, our weak eyes
bitter with their nakedness.

The shadow-wrinkled lake slides past,
folding its chills into each other.
Is it for you I stare, my lost one?

An instant ago, on the crest of the ice,
we were lovers, skimming the glistening
skin of snow like dragonflies,

our eyes fixed on each other, each
wanting to be seen in
the lamplight of the other's glance.

Now I fill my gaze
with the stripped body of rock,
the glacial face so charged with its own

will to annihilation
it needn't even check its blank reflection
in the blank face of the lake.

Memory Fails

1.
The frame so intricate and rich
without a picture,

the tall walls of the house
surrounding emptiness,

the eyes without pupils,
the breasts that have no milk, no nipples:

you sit
beside yourself

in the dead hotel,
white spread, white sheets,

blank mahogany bedstead,
and ask for old Polaroids

of a face that evidently never
existed: the petals

have lost their flower, the air
has shed its unseen

weight, its once
emphatic temperature.

2.
Why do the black ducks on the stony coast
fly toward summer?
They move like splashes of ink
across the horizon,
as though their motion were a sentence
aching with meaning.

3.
Past midnight. The rented lamp
spills light on the ashtray,

the pillow is thick with forbidden sleep,
words haunt the corridors.

The philosopher in his tweeds
has gone back to the college gardens.

You sit by
yourself, you'd better

try to remember the code
that unlocks the pillow.

4.

The Pacific stings, licks, sucks.
You say you want its cold tongues
to open your throat, you say
you want to swallow

those glittering voices
that might tell you
what the heat claimed last summer, what
the darkness lifted and poured

as you turned in the light bed
toward the one you loved,
as you embraced and were embraced
by the one you have forgotten,

as you moved within that white, that warm
that salt-sweet body
with no need for words
or memory.

Some Definitions

1. Aperitif

Take a cup of breath,
stir in a silence, stones on a shore,

twirl, whip—
add glinting, minnows,

groan of oars,
and beat in,

and beat in
the darkness that creeps from the inland mountains,

the darkness that clots the eye of the tiger,
the rat, the pig.

Beat in one clump,
then another.

2. *These Old Keys*

innocent, brazen,
refuse to say *no*, to nod
to circumstance.

                 Instead,
they jostle, clash,
toward darkness:

now their teeth
bite down on the tender
jars of the locks,

they gnaw
at morsels of silence,
open a few more

bloody doors.

3. *October Cobwebs*

screen the garden in the late
heat, the lowering
light, like lines

to nowhere, nets
of glimmer toward whose
savage unseen

centers
weak flies strut
or stumble,

and like flags
of dissolution,
each one lovely in its tired

silver
as the loosened
hold of leaves

or dark emerging
bulk of trunks
and branches

over which the story of
a thousand disappearing
tenants

seems still,
          now,
to move and breathe.

4. Basil

A question the box of earth
still asks the kitchen,

as in green blades
of Liguria, green

spears of the watery
forests of Thailand,

peppery keen
airs of August,

as in wise king
do not fade,

as in a pot of,
where the lover's head

explodes into new
ideas, *as in*

chop the loss finely,
add salt and stew

and halo the old charred
grandmother stove,

as in what to do
with the last

three stained tomatoes
hung on the vine.

5. *Fog on the Coast*

Lid of thin
milk across the light,
skin of mist

above the waters,
weight
of vacancy pressing

against the eyes, great
shapeless
throat of silence

swallowing everything:
here's where
trawlers disappear, black

bluffs melt, ambitious
summer houses
step into nowhere

and only
the closeup has a chance,
the mouse and her grain,

the jagged
pebble, the nettle
standing its ground

among a few spare
outlines of sound—
            the faint

hint of a gull, the sea
still hungrily
thumping its table.

6. Pumpkin

Last fat in the elegiac
light, last
round among the stalks,

last creased
dwarf of color
heating the stubble,

final
bulge of orange
swelling

above forgetful
grasses, pondering
pulp and seed—

say
how the shadows
fatten too at nightfall,

tell how
finally
all growth is monstrous,

as if the truth of age
were gross accumulation, weight
not withering,

an ornery
deformity the fated
end of ripeness.

7. Enormous Wind

buffets the sea, creasing the blue-
green shine, rock-polishing
the dazzle cast by billows
of light, by bursts of sudden
uncoloring, unpatterning

the waves that just an hour ago
were staid and shapely
in their mild arc and spray,
their falling hopes.
their rising expectations.

8. Mexican Sage

Purple but minimal,
as if the curled-up
hardly daring petals

were so embarrassed
by that thread of reddish
pink desire pumping

through the long coarse
stems they ride
that they'd grow smaller

rather than grow at all,
yet nonetheless they
have to keep on

beading the gray-green
quiet with this
humiliating

flush, have to
love the touch of
touch, the quiver

in tiny silence,
have to be
plush in the cold.

9. November Afternoon

Now of all the bloom that loved the meadow
only the nettles are left to shine,

their purple stare
bedded in nails, their neighbors

chaff for the wind,
dirt on the fur of the world,

their thrusts of thistledown
quilting nearly everything

nearby a blur
of silver-gray.

And the nights chill, thicken, open
enormous arms.

And the grandparents sink deeper
into the spinning center

of what is done, what is gone.
And December

wheels forward, alert and brisk,
unfolding a small pale sky

in which the solstice
hovers like a hawk.

10. *Spoon*

No bowl but only the smallest
curve to scoop to
taste to grasp

with a glint of silver
still in the tarnish
as if a spoonful of sorrow

makes the sugar go
into the twittering leaves, the sky so
broken with streaks of fading

there must be a ladle
to lap it up, to lave
the bodies of trees and hills,

but no, there's only, there's
anyway, just this one
blackening spoon.

11. *Leaves*

Was there ever anything a speaking
body had or could that could

compare with these thin
silks, these fluttering

slices of feeling-the-light,
nerve endings of flare and glow?

Past midnight: the witching
bath of the cold

is everywhere but not a flicker not
a flinch of discontent

troubles the small
eccentric shadows.

Then a crisp commotion,
falling, rising, settling

into something else.
Quickness flickering

through the air, quickness sighing
Goodbye to the old edges,

the angled gold that bit the wind
that ate the sun.

And now the sky stands up naked,
disclosing its plans.

12. December

In the blue-bleak underground kitchen
the fire has just about
gone out and the grandchildren
squat by the stove,

hoping for a last crust.
But their crone of a *nonna*
lies down in ice, face of stone
turned to the stony wall.

She has hidden her treasure
under a pillow of cold,
scrolled her will
in a tube of bone.

They can wait till I'm dead, she says.
Then they'll find out what they're getting!

13. *After*

the prizes, the speeches,
the photographers in noisy bars,

after the smashed glass in the restaurant,
the embrace on the balcony, the swerving traffic,

beyond the valley,
the three dark ponds,

the lanes with their swaying
stands of lilies,

hike the long slope
to the ice cap,

crouch by the crust,
drink the shimmer

of its many breasts,
worship its pearl veil,

its sweat of mist.

14. Dark Blue

To write every night in the dark blue
book of grief. To write every.
Night. To write night,
its letters edged with half the shades

of dark blue in the blue
black span
of the milky spine
of the galaxy:

       is this
the thought
the slick roads stipulate
at dusk when the clock skids back

and the sleet slides open
its clattering veils
and there is the sudden
dark blue

book of shining?

15. Trunk

There is what is
given and thick
and hardly knows
itself, knows only

down and *up* and knows
in the numbness
nothing more but
still and *yet*, and still, yet,

down and up,
the grip of the digging,
the slow accretion
into what might

still and yet
be light.

16. *One Pine Cone in the Fire*

seems to refuse to burn
forever, scaly and gray,
a dinosaur egg, an arrogant nut
that won't give up.
                    Then,

thin skins of flame
peel from its side, it tilts,
sighs, settles into terrible red:
it's the haunch of a bird,
energy rising like cries of fear

as the raccoon on delicate claws
sways toward the branch,
it's the nest where the field mouse cowered
till the cat caught it,
it's the one feather the wind

left on the doorstep
in the wild night outside
where the moon is full and blue clouds
are sifting apart like ashes and black pines
shudder toward the sky.

17. *Calvados*

Heat of the apple, soul
of the wish inspiriting
the tree, fall

of sweetness flaming
away: here's
maybe the final

ghost of *full* and *ripe*
in a lucky punctual
goblet, shining

naked to taste,
humming how now
in the garden the last

stalks yearn, last
briefs of color
claim and jostle

and won't give up.

But the tree so silent,
the picnic table sputtering out.

What strolls in the grove?
Go sit on the battered
chaise the former owner

left still warm.
Go sit and sip.
And listen.

Forget to weep.

Objet Trouvé

Something put me in this place where I am
and I am not I:

and there's a yellow light, a great light
bearing down on me, a wheel of heat,

and black and white in subtle turns,
the print of cryptic characters—

the *Times*, the *News*—around me,
and a clot of sticky stuff that clamps me to a space

I never thought would happen,
where enormous lines

cross, cling, and hold me still—
and still I'm drifting, drifting out of

what you call a picture, out of your collage,
and hanging here in silence

while the watchers gawk,
I wriggle out of the bloody glue,

and move,
and gather speed.

Outside the design it's blue,
it's green and blue.

There's wild iris in a meadow, the toss of a sea
that's nobody's museum.

Faster and faster, I'm tearing out of the frame.
If you tell me who I am,

if you tell me my name,
I'll imagine you back.

I might even try to love you
if you tell me what I'm flying into.

After Long Rain,

when I walk through the windbreak
I feel words rising from the wet ground

as if in this sudden hush some mild heat
trembled from the buried center,

or as if the earth around old roots
had washed away to let odd colonies—

rings of fungus, circles of iris—
scramble up from soil and stone. . . .

I have to hold out my hands, spread
my fingers like divining rods.

Even the skin of my palms
hears the new growth humming.

Is this what it means to be
the one who has to speak,

the one they sent alone into the forest
to find the wild mushrooms?

Omens

A sky electric with geese.
My sudden pulse.

You're coming. Back.
The rumor of your return

bearing down like the great wheels
of a jet descending.

You to whom a glittering
splash of sparrow,

a shriek of jay,
are minor portents.

You who have never entirely gone away.
You who have never been completely here.

You're coming.
Your enormous baggage of lights and clouds

littering the mountains,
your shadowy ladders

unscrolling sentences
step after step.

Even the least shiver of my breathing
seized and used

in the shrill wind of your arrival.

Epithalamion

—for Ruth Schorer Loran and in memory of Erle Loran

Sun soaking the deck, the August meadow
dazed with noon, even the dome

of sky, the scoop of sea
still in a trance of heat,

               and my new
love has gone to see the seals:

meditating theorems
I'll never understand,

he's traveling the cliff-top path
my husband used to walk,

maybe marveling
as the dead one did

at the thrift of all the tiny wild
creatures—skinny daisies, half transparent

gnats and inchling
lizards, sprouting flitting swooping

through the lupine—
            and maybe now,

just as my dead man did,
he's counting seals, rogue

bachelors, nursing mothers, blotchy
quivering babies, and admiring how

they love the rocks and salt alike, the hungry
plunge through foam, the languorous

nap on granite,
                    and maybe without even

noticing the light that makes him smile a bit
(while he ponders odd equations)

he's moved as I am by the silent
marriages that urge the meadow

into bloom, its whole exhausted body
rising the way the tall New Zealand

tree fern my dead husband planted
looms above the boards I sit on,

looms, leans and tenderly unfolds
frond after feathery frond as it weds itself

again,
        again

to the incalculable
sway of air, the sheer

luxury of sun.

III

When She Was Kissed by the Mathematician

—for D.G.

The dyad is a source of number. The first increase and change results in the dyad and in the doubling of the monad. . . . It is analogous to matter and to everything perceptible. Among the virtues, they liken it to courage, for it has already made an advance.

—ANATOLIUS, *On the Decad*

When She Was Kissed by the Mathematician

The morning after the night she was
kissed by the mathematician,

she woke with a new
intelligence:

        that words are spaces
I can fill, she thought,

with values of my own
(and as and at my wish)

may be a proposition
warm and lively as a kiss—

and that this x *can equal* y
propounds a why I just might

someday answer
if I choose and will.

Rain had washed
the affable deck all night,

its invisible equations
echoing the lucid lemmas

spoken by the mathematician
through his musing kisses.

Gravity floated off
in the dawn sun,

and she embraced
a hypothesis she'd long forgotten:

Energy, she declared,
as she bounded out of bed,

amasses in my sentence,
bold as a theorem, old as light.

Beyond her study door
the garden bloomed with glittering proofs.

Her Response to His Theorem

Squares within squares, triangles
in triangles, and other infinite
analyses of forms:
the mathematician's subtle propositions
cut things up and slyly down.

That night he was the vector,
she the matrix—a common enough
example of romance, with lowered lamps
casting a mild geometry
across the bed, the quilt, the kisses.

Capably his fingers theorized
archaic charms and new delights.
"Oh, what are you doing to me now?"
she gasped,
half passing out.

"Just showing interest in you, sweetheart,"
he answered, tough as
Humphrey Bogart,
while he tenderly, adroitly,
mapped each body part.

She Grapples with Operations Research

> *. . . the by now famous problem of the jeep . . . concerns a jeep which is able to carry enough fuel to travel a distance* d, *but is required to cross a desert whose distance is greater than* d *(for example* 2d). *It is to do this by carrying fuel from its home base and establishing fuel depots at various points along its route so that it can refuel as it moves further out. . . . [But] in general, the more jeeps one sends across, the lower fuel consumption per jeep.*
> —David Gale, "The Jeep Once More or
> Jeeper by the Dozen"

The mathematician is crossing the desert,
his fine high features creased with thought.

One tank of fuel at *this* depot, another stashed at that.
How many caches needed in between?

She worries. It's all too Zeno for her liking.
And what if he insists on the Sahara?

No, he promises, he'll only try the kindlier
Mojave this time, with its rainstruck buds and rare

new blossoms rising while his jeep,
his squad of jeeps, moves slowly on the trip

through sand, through quarks and quirks of sand,
their particles an endless series

as she waits and hates his danger.
The mathematician crosses, curses, blesses

the infinite regressions of the desert:
and the desert sun storms down like thunder, like a roar

of light against his beard, his temples
clenched with calculations

and desire.
                    At stated stations,

palms, dates, springs of comfort
will appear. And there he'll prudently

sequester further energies.
Blank sky and melting gold, keen blade

of lemmas roaring through his engine.
She stands on the sidelines in the shade.

She stirs a pitcher of gin and lemonade.
Astute, her body manufactures

leafy murmurs as she turns herself
into a crystal dish of peaches.

The mathematician is crossing the desert,
crossing, journeying past Zeno, past the infinite.

She wants to be the first
oasis that he reaches.

He Issues Commands

Midnight. The bedside clock
decrees its own assumptions.
The mathematician murmurs, half asleep,
commanding shadows and definitions.

Let K *be a field,*
let Y *be a non-singular matrix,*
let K[x] *be a ring of polynomials*
over a field. . . .

Under the tousled covers,
she sighs, listens, tries
to piece his words together.
Let K *be a field.*

His body is a field, simmering.
She wants to hide in its
wild grasses, slip into
its stream of sleep.

Let K *be a field,*
let K[x] *be a ring of polynomials*
holding her close.
Let the bed be a field,

a nighttime meadow mouthing
dark equations, singular
matrices. Let its kisses
be long as midsummer dusk.

Later, let there be light,
let the solution of dawn
be a unique, an
irrational sun.

He Discusses Gravity

The attraction of one body to another—
as, the apple to the Earth, the feather
to the rock, the leaning tower
to its shadow traced on Pisan stone:

he explains this undercover
in the simmering darkness where their bodies
reach and touch, gravely
attracted. It's the mass

that does it, heart of the matter, mass
plus nearness. The closer the body
of the other, the more the body
of the one craves touch.

                As now,
she knows she's falling
rapidly toward him
like that apocryphal apple

plummeting toward the grass at Newton's feet,
or like the rock that Galileo dropped
one curious day in Pisa, or even—
especially—like the feather

that the wise man said would fall
(all else being equal)
as fast and fierce as rock
toward the desirous body of the ground.

After He Expounds the Theorem
of the Different Infinities

Half the night sleepless, dreaming infinities—
the countable set and the unaccountable—

she listens to his breathing, sometimes
even, placid and perfectly

divisible, the way she imagines
certain numbers are,

sometimes stopped by odd
irregular murmurs, listens and counts

his breaths, his unintelligible words
as if she wrapped a rosary of integers

around her wrists, his wrists, linking them both
in the smaller infinity, the kind you can count

and maybe comprehend,
the one that Zeno scorned.

His chest with its mane of gray
rises and falls as she counts, crawls nearer,

wishing he'd explain again or else
embrace her, silence this abacus

of prayer that ticks in her head:
O God, whatever you are, let this one

be—and the bed swells
in the heat, in the dark, and the single

sheet that holds them close
winds round and round like the great

enfolding spaces through which arrows
fly and breaths and prayers

on their eccentric route
toward Zeno's black incalculable target.

Long Division

Switch on the gooseneck lamp!
Fix its small hot stare on all
the axioms, the algorithms, the wary
probabilities:

that light and heat
go into the shell of emptiness
only so many (so few!)
times, that absence

multiplies itself
again and over, carrying unknown
powers, that chance
is fatal, history unlikely—

No wonder in the course of days unequal
to each other he forgets
to love, his fingers gnarl
around a pencil, scribbling *minus*,

and the gasping propositions
fail, the intricate equations
of desire and need
no longer hold.

Night after night she watches
in the dark as the mathematician
curls himself into the horizontal
eight of an infinity

that's self-complete, wants
no one, nothing, nothing
solid anyway,
and morning after morning

watches, waking,
as the dark divides in tiny
bands of color, quickly
flashing across their bodies,

quickly gone.

They Debate Triangles and Medians

That they *are* is obvious to him,
remarkable to her.
She grants the points, their dark

necessity, each a moment brimming
with its own being—
and the lines, well, given points

and given time,
no doubt there must be lines,
those fateful journeyings

from here to there, from this to that.
But the vertices where journeys meet,
the angles, wide or narrow, yearning for closure

and then letting go—
aren't these, she asks, unlikely
as the medians that cling together

at the center of each triangle,
knotting altitudes and perpendiculars
into a single web of possibility?

And maybe Euclid got it halfway right:
in luminous sections, intersections,
everything is joined and rational,

at least for a while,
as if somebody had suddenly conjectured yes,
it *can* make sense—

and the triangles and medians
of you and me and them
last and glow till one by one

the fastenings unclasp
and that which must be linear
sheds the comforts of shape,

each line going its lonely distance
to the non-Euclidean place
where parallels diverge in darkness.

He Explains the Book Proof

The shadowy clatter of the café
frames the glittering doorway.

A white cup and a blue bowl
inscribe pure shapes on the table.

The mathematician says, *Let's turn the pages
and find the proof in the book of proofs.*

He says, *It's as if it's already there,
somewhere just outside the door,*

as if by sitting *zazen* in a coffeehouse,
someone could get through or get "across,"

or as if the theorems had already all
been written down on sheer

sheets of the invisible,
and held quite still,

so that to think hard enough
is simply to read and to recall—

the way the table remembers the tree,
the bowl remembers the kiln.

IV

At Cleopatra Bay

At Cleopatra Bay,

where the great yachts pause, and the smaller craft,
the Turkish boatmen say
She stopped here once,

and I struggle to see the fire of her barge
standing among the outboard motors,
the parasailors, the day-trippers,

as if she and her straining mariners
might drift from the Mediterranean sky
englobed in gold, or better still

explode from the cold
where the sunken cities loll,
her handsome imperious face,

with its lithe cruel brows, tipped eyes,
lips that taste of bitter leaves,
unmoved by our futuristic engine-grind.

Three thousand years—a splash of centuries!—
and the bay is still the same,
the rocky coves where dabs of fish

stitch little seams of light and dark,
the feathery southern pines
that stoop above the streams they shadow

as if searching for new images
through mirrors of themselves,
the spit of sunstruck island where perhaps

she might have walked an hour among
trivial grasses, armguards flashing
as she took the measure of her men—

Then Ahmet breaks the spell:
"Everywhere you turn around here
there's another place they swear she stopped:

every other inlet brags
it's Cleopatra bay!"
Ubi sunt:

she was everywhere, *is* nowhere.
There are no footfalls
on the vanished stair,

the drowned landing.

Sorrow

Five years after your funeral
in the hot flat Sacramento valley,
a cosmopolite, journeying, journeying
and dozing over the pages of an old Conrad
you left behind (I took along),
I wake to my sorrow on the deck
of a tall-masted *gulet* among the Lycian tombs,
the sunken cities, of Kekova Bay.

Five days this week I've lived in the turquoise
Turkish air, the Mediterranean air
that glitters like a wall of Izmir tiles,
among smart young European traders, wise-
cracking along the ancient shipping lanes—
viz., Why did Constantinople fall, and why
did—*what?*—survive, and how do we "forecast"
the wealth the future might not bring?

Regression analyses, functions, factors,
jostle among *dolmades* and honeycakes.
These slim cosmopolites—you'd call them "kids"—
care, if scoffingly, what stocks will rise,
what nations fall, as if each stop in time
were a *Sorry!* square and the thousand
sunken cities (you're in one of them)
just pieces in a comic game.

The coasts of history recede, expand,
collapse. Great tides engulf the tanned
backgammon players on the pier.
And now the water skiers come, curving
and swooping like gulls across the sorrow
that clasped the bay just now. . . .
And now the captain ratchets the anchor up.
And now the boys untie our lines.

Unmoored, we're back at sea—
a scoop of polished wood set free among
blue leagues of salt, and journeying,
journeying toward Fethiye, toward Göcek, toward
the heaped-up darkness of the Taurus mountains,
then back to the place we came from,
the city that will no doubt never again
call itself Byzantium.

Shelling Beans Outside Pollenca

Dying to be devoured, the beans
plunge from the pod to the pot,
whole generations linked
in every long slim creamy-yellow
scarlet-splotched canoe.

God made them to be eaten—
built their hulls to dangle, crash,
split, smash, deliver each one
naked and clutching its starch
into the maw of dirt or rock.

Two fields away the animals
choir their utter oblivion:
sheep-groan, rooster-scream, dog-howl
swell above the giant insect-
buzz of the ground.

And how imperious the mountains are,
vaunting their indigestible granite!
How stately the fandango of pines
whose needles haven't been shredded yet!
And the silvery olives, picturesque, antique—

how indifferent to the doom of brine, of mulch,
how alert and feathery
their tiptoe toward a roaring sun
you'll never feel or love
or see again.

Aurora Borealis

—*for D.*

37,000 feet up, halfway to Paris, halfway
from San Francisco, and though the time zone's
indeterminate, the night that stands its sullen
shaft of ice over the peaks of Labrador
is unequivocal—

minus sixty degrees
less than six inches from the toasty cabin
where we curl in crumpled rows.
And you're trying to doze,
and I'm trying to concentrate on Bashō.

Narrow the road to the deep north,
and perilous the flyway
over the tilting top of the world,
the ice that clenches itself against the light
miles down and down—

the *no*
of the cold that wants to grow its own
eternity from here to Paris
and back to the Golden Gate
we started from.

My love, my dead man told me
about that cold: he said our grounds
would all be frozen to the core
if the oceans weren't salt.
It's the salt, he said, that lets us live.

The sea won't freeze, won't stop,
won't give itself up to the *no*
that strikes from the sky,
Aurora that would chill the blood
of the whole world if it could!

But love, our blood won't freeze,
and our hot tears glitter
with a brilliant *yes*
that hurts the way the ocean
hurts a wound:

I want that *yes*
to carry us east toward
daybreak over the deep
north, noon
in the city of light.

Last Sunday at *Les Grands Eaux Musicales*

Versailles stank, as if its recycled waters
jetted from the rotting bones
of rotten-to-the-core courtiers,

or as if the queen's expensive sewage
had been sewn into the centers
of a dozen hidden tanks the way

her plaything sheep had shit
sewn up inside them, the better to guard
the milky hands of lady milkmaids.

(Says my daughter's guidebook, *puce*
was a color invented by couturiers
to hide the fleas on courtly satin.)

Now stench flings up from the laps of gilded naiads
and cascades among the colonnades on a lawn
once thought *parfait* for a mild *repas*,

while from their artful camouflage
above the heads of the ambling rabble,
dozens of speakers relay Lully

to the ghosts of Louis, Louis, and Louis,
as if to say, *The King is dead!*
Long live his royal stink!

Why, then, at the lowest verge of the garden
do we watch a little wet-eyed
as the last bronze Apollo

surges out of the sewage,
archaic charioteer, his horses thundering
up from the marble pit, his fat-faced outriders

blowing their veils of dissolute water
skyward in showers of light
coming noisily higher and brighter . . . ?

Autumn, Como

1. Olives

They've cut the grass in the olive grove.
A floor of pallor, close and prickly,
coats the slopes above the lake,

and the wind spins off the water,
hissing, nagging, repeating
its old dissatisfaction,

its grudge against solids.
Whirl the world apart!
The loose dead stems that once were grass

ride lonely tides, widening
circles. Hard and green,
flocks of olives

clamp to their branches,
fat with the cold new life
they have to hold for three more months.

2. *Poets*

The poet who searches the hillside now
trots after those staggering Englishmen—
spindly Shelley facing down the wind,
Keats, shoulder-high to his comrades, coughing
blood into language.

Down by the lake the small gnats
mourn no more:
                  glittering specks
bob and flee,
too dumb for words.

3. *Bread*

Outside Bellagio, above the unchanging
fact of the lake,

the leaves of the liquidambar
spurt scarlet as Vermont,

and a scratch of smoke is in the air,
and sparse twigs quiver

across the plain still veil of gray
that might be lake or sky:

and along the steady blank of water
food of the dead

basks behind glass in every *paneficio:*
round smooth *fave dei morti*

(the bakers call them *morbida*)
and sugared *pane dei morti,*

soft as the underfrills of mushrooms—
beans and bread to fill the still white bodies

stacked in berths in cluttered villages
along the shore, beans for the mouths of the dead,

bread of October
they can clasp in their long pale

silent hands.

4. *Wind*

All afternoon, all night, tatters of sky
claw at the shutters.

Morning:
          step of a leaf on gravel,

step of a twig
on the path past the fountain.

Some invisible man
runs rings around the villa,

and a tide of sorrow
streams where he goes.

5. Castle

Today a stillness.
Fog squats in the moldering
castle on the point

where no one is left to tell
how the painted galley with its sword-sharp
ice-crusted prow

came headlong down the lake,
how the bones of the sailors
curved, clasped, lifted, fitted

arrows to bows, bowstrings
to skulls, how the fine shafts
soared or pierced or fell

on what, for whom, in which
misty cause.

6. *Evening Rain*

A rainy twilight, clouds
close and tragic as old
women

      plucking at passersby,
whispering their wrongs.

A thicket of white umbrellas
blooms in the tall white jar
by the door of the villa,

but those who cross the lake
in the late boat

pass through layers of tender
moisture, float between
water and water,

while in the chilly cabin
the ones who have forgotten vanity

stare at the lake in the sky
through their own
          unseen outlines.

7. Morning Rain

Rain like lace in the cypresses,
the day of the dead gone by, the town
shut up for winter,

                    and the ferries
hanging, desultory, in a mist
that mingles sky and lake and mountain

as if no *fiat* ever pierced the chaos
from which earth, air, water
once were drawn.

                  Groan of an unseen
tractor grinding up a long invisible
hill, trill of an unknown bird,

clatter of trucks
through a drift of milky steam.
Then a pause, a breathlessness.

The vast cold mass of gray
just touches the shore, just grazes
the cold massif,

just lightly,
          patiently,
waiting to be a lake again.

Notes in Provence

1. Dante

At Les Baux, where the placid ranks of olives
erupt into stone, where the sun plunges
in and down

to cleave the peaks and the mild.
fields shatter,
there was the secret, there the green

trembled and tore itself open,
exposing the burning
gut of justice, the princes

twisting in agony
under it all, the naked
ladies clapped in lascivious

flame, the groaning
serfs and satyrs heaving below
the meadow that looked so kind,

its million starry eyes
blinking and glowing, its cloak
of innocent glisten, its feathers

of thyme, its tender prickles,
held close but just
not close enough

to hide the rocky
horns of the traitor, the infamous
gorge, the fierce eternally

grinding teeth.

2. Van Gogh

Each afternoon the surging fields invent Van Gogh again:
his green mind glittering in the trees—the flame

and flail of poplars, dark thick
pulse of cypresses: his blue

mind mad as sky
that reaches beyond the edge of green,

beyond the toss of grain, scorch of stone,
and shrieks with light:

his yellow mind
exploding orchards, plumy grasses,

curling coiling spiraling vines, tiny
unseen eyes of grapes: his black

mind pawing the dust of long unraveling
roads the way the humped black bull locked in an endless

corrida at Arles
bellows his animal grief as slim pale two-

dimensional beings flit across the tattered
canvas of his mind.

Catedral at Tlacolula

No space left empty, not a scroll
or curlicue unused, even the frames of scribbles
are scribbled on, as if the builders
had to keep busy every second,
as if to cease from motion
would mean lapsing into the glare
that threatens color, sickens shape. . . .

Explosions of artifice! Rocket
bursts of plane geometry! The whole
vault of wall and ceiling
vaunts a history of squiggles,
conquering the dust of the *alta plana*!
And cargoes of martyrs incomprehensibly
unloaded at every port!

Locked in glass boxes, the lounging saints
brood on torment, insouciant
as *gringos* contemplating lunch,
or now and then an eager one
leans into the wall of pain, mouth agape,
the way a specimen bird, flouncing in its cage,
might yearn toward its next feeding.

But the tiny virgin in her black brocade,
mailed with mirrors reflecting
everything and nothing,
stares beyond saints and squiggles
into the glittering toy heaven
her doll baby promises
with his flat black Zapotec eyes.

Trionfo del Morte

—in memory of E.L.G., 1930–1991

1. Dream

It's 1997, I'm still myself,
and I wake up wet-eyed
in the strange hotel.

The birds of Tuscany, voluble Italians,
ring my window.

You left and you left no number.

All night I called.
All night and there was no answer.
All night the operator knew nothing.

Baby poplars
file in arrogant squares
along the muddy Alberi

where in-between-time swallows
stitch and unstitch the sky
in sweet parabolas

and the tremulous monk, last
guardian of San Vivaldo
cries *alleluia* in his cracked old voice.

Stubbornly ripening toward infinity
in your distant
numberless compartment,

you have forgotten to love me.

2. Cookbook

My lover's grandson the teenage would-be cook
worships the photos of *abbondanza,*

so much deeper than those watery frescoes in Pisa
where industrious Franciscans defy the *Trionfo del Morte*

as if they could hoe and harvest and bake
eternal life into its proper place.

Take the salt from the bread, counsels the cookbook,
crush the gold from the olive, the scarlet from the grape,

the blood from the hare, the boar, the lark!
Reap and store, simmer and preserve!

In his corner the grandfather turns away
as the oldest monk turned from harvest to altar.

Grief is the recipe,
sorrow the food.

The *pappardelle* are not enough.
They will not cover the stone table on the *terrazza*.

3. *Museum*

Scenes from the golden world—angels
with the wings of peacocks, courtiers
in the guise of angels,

unending slabs of God
splayed on intersecting
slabs of wood,

and the skull of a saint
in a crystal box lit up
with swirls of gilt:

death was the engine that drove the golden world
to the edge of hell,
death

primping on the flowery sward,
preening in the palace garden,
death in its triumph

tearing the tiny souls
out of the mouths of merchants,
death frescoing the ceilings

with its cherubs,
death adorable in radiance
weaving its thread of ice

into the holy vestments,
catching the last trickles of martyrs
in the stone chalice

of the museum where baffled tourists
turn again and again to the mystifying
pages of the guidebook, the barely legible

labels under the hangings.

Hurtigruten*

1. Alesund: North

(To the west you can see the open Atlantic Ocean and the islands
with their ancient settlements.)

The doors fly open and in flow
the skeptical airs of the north:

damp air of the troll cave,
mushroom breath, bog wind,

ice breeze bruising early
certainties, asserting freezing

nots—
not south, with its silken

collisions, its tumbles of gold,
nor west, so simple

in waves of yearning,
nor east, whose doughty

dawns circle like gulls,
insisting that is and possible are one,

*Hurtigruten means Coastal Express. All epigraphs are taken from Erling
Storrusten, Hurtigruten: The World's Most Beautiful Sea Voyage (Bergen: ERA-Trykk
AS, 1996).

but north, and strict
in rigorous doubt,

and now the steep houses
huddled in smoke

hunch against questions
that hoot like great gray geese,

and now the lips of the cliff
open and beckon,

and now a tall white sky
stoops to the shadow

that follows the aged sailor set
adrift today in a single wistful

meadow, smiling his random
ice floe of a smile.

2. Ornes: Midnight Sun

(All along the coast, you'll find former trading posts which remain untouched by progress.)

and broad daylight has a special meaning:
like the French *plein ciel*, daylight
spreads its heavenly apricot *confiture*

far and wide across the righteous houses
that would sleep if they could
but must wake in the fat flash

of a sunset that settles in
like a beaming cousin
come for a too-long visit,

and the ice on the gables gets all helplessly
rosy as if seduced despite
its austere principles,

while travelers from darker places
look out in delight
at the edge of town

where the still ordinary
ordinary is
what really surprises—

a steamer unloading lunch for a giant,
a flag saluting, a little sheepishly,
as a boy in a shiny anorak

rides a bicycle around
and around the wharf
in widening circles.

3. Salt Fjord: Arctic

(The strait is only negotiable two hours after high and low tide.)

North of Auden's north and the north
of the sagas, even the meditative
north of Rilke—

north where the spectrum
vanishes, and memory—its vast
harvests of color—,

north where minutes are only latitude,
and the tongue of the traveler
begins to trill despite itself,

The people who come of this ice
cannot be like us, surely
they speak in cries like seabirds,

surely they have toes as fierce
as the roots of pines that tighten
around sheer rock,

surely they creak in the wind
like old ships passing the skerries
as they journey, forgetting themselves,

among great boulders of absence.

4. *Lyngstuva: One* A.M.

(Beware of Lyngstuva, a mountain protruding 390 m from the sea
between Ulls Fjord and Lyngen Fjord.)

The exhaustion of the inexhaustibly
beautiful!

       —the effort it asks
with its ceaseless

look and *listen*, its imperious
call for scrutiny—as here,

this crag, with its difficult
partitions, how they shine,

as if from within, as if
a translucent new geometry

might form right here,
among sea and sky

and stone in the unwavering
pupil of a sun we

have to keep looking at
hour on hour just as

framed in the ice
of indefatigable difference

it has to keep looking
back at us.

5. Trollfjorden: Gerda

(To the south, the peak of Trolltindan soars 1,045–1,084 m above sea level, and its sheer sides pose a permanent threat of rock falls. To the north is Blafjellet. . . . To the west is the lake of Trollfjordvatnet, filled with chunks of ice even during the summer.)

"Then as we went farther north
it grew brighter and colder

in the enormous
gaze of the ice

and I who once was little Gerda
in my land as blonde as cream

cried out toward where
you aged in the embrace that was

no longer snow but fixed like a cliff
in its greed for you,

I cried, I cried out twice
for little Kay, who was my

mate in what might have been
a meadow, and all the aching

buzzing gold,
all the buttercups and thistles,

all the night moths and dawn eggs
in the meadow of old

Gerda, gripping her twisted stick,
cried out for old Kay,

whose naked mouth yawned wider
and wider now

in an O
that could swallow nothing."

6. *Nordkappbanken: Open Sea*

that will not freeze
though the snow fields creep to the shore
and the crawling glaciers

glint and lure
that will not freeze
in the Arctic dark

when the great
lights seethe and flash
and the humped winds

plunge against black
hooks of rock and stranger
backs that neither

flinch nor grunt
that will not freeze
in the clasp of polar

ice that hisses
across abandoned
nests and bones

that will not freeze
that pulses with fish
that pulse with life

that streams invisibly
on and on
again and on

V

From *Ghost Volcano* (1995)

Kissing the Bread

1.
and the fields inside it.
The winter of the crumb, the iron
hoe hacking the furrow,
the hiss of grain in the wind.

The priest in the crust
says *kiss,* says
In nomine Domine,
bless, kiss.

2.

My mother in the four by seven
yellow kitchen in Queens,
pressing her lips to half a
loaf of day-old challah, the food
of someone else's sabbath,
before dropping it into the red and white
step-on can:
her mother the Sicilian midwife
taught her, taught all nine,
to kiss the bread before you
throw it away.

        Why?
Non so. You kiss it, like
crossing yourself before a crisis, before
the train leaves the station,
before the baby falls,
startled, into a sudden
scorch of air.

3.

No. No doubt
not that. But instead
Dickinson's "the Instead."
They were full of terrible
accurate sentiment,
those old Italian ladies in the kitchen—
crones, with witch hairs haloing
their chins, with humps and staggers
and nodes of bone ringing their fingers.

Kissing the bread was kissing
the carrion that was the body
of every body, the wrist

of daughter and husband, the crook'd
arm of the mother, the stone
fist of the father.

Kissing *goodbye*,
saying the daily
goodbye, the skeptical
god be with you
as the long loaf sank into ashes,
as the oven sputtered its
merciless complaint.

4.

They were kissing the corn god, you say?
Kissing the host, the guest,
the handsome one who grows
so tall and naked
in the August grove?

But what if they were mocking him,
mocking the crust that stiffened, the crumbs
that staled and scattered?

    You thought,
bread, that your magic
salts were eternal, that your holy
taste was your final shape,
but see, you were wrong:
I bid you goodbye, my tongue
gives you a last touch, my teeth
renounce you.

5.

But no again: my mother's kiss
was humble, the mortified
kiss of guilt—*I can use you
no longer*—and the kiss
of dread: *what will I do, challah,
pumpernickel, rye, baguette, sweet white,
thick black, when you
are gone?*

      And the kiss, I think
I thought she meant,
of sorrow, as if kissing
the bread is kissing
the crows that fly low over
fields we never saw in Queens,
the blurry footprints
between long rows of wheat,
the blank sun roaring overhead.

We stood in the Jackson Heights kitchen.
The white 1940s Kelvinator
whirred, no comment, and strips of
city snow crisscrossed the window.

I was eight and baffled.

*If an angel should be flying by
when you make that face, she said,
you'll be stuck with it forever.*

October 6, 1992:
Seattle, Looking for Mount Rainier

The housekeeper says she doesn't know.
Limping, gray-haired, dwarfed, she's cleaned these rooms
for fifteen years, but she's still not sure.

Over there—she points to a cutout line of hills—
the Olympics maybe.
                            An hour later,

it surges out of the clouds, mystic as Valhalla,
just opposite the spot
where she thought perhaps I'd find it.

Three months after you died, Susan and I
flew over the gasp of the peak
in a tiny frightening Cessna.

I forgot the lacy petals in the meadows outside
Paradise Lodge where we picnicked
en famille in 1980.

Stared at the grooved grim face.
My husband's face, I told her. Dead
and gigantic and frozen in reproach.

Ten minutes wide, centuries long.
I wanted to fall, I had fallen
into the hissing crevices, the lanes of ice

where I knew you wandered, shivering
even in your Irish sweater, your old blue parka.
No end to the scowl of the mountain that was you,

no end to the screech of the Valkyrie,
dragging you past the ledges of light
into yourself.

        Now,
distant as our innocent goodbye,
it's a mirage on the horizon:

ghost volcano.
Dwellers in this city
say *sometimes you see it,*

sometimes you don't.

February 11, 1992:
At the Art Institute of Chicago

The Van Gogh roomscape draws me
with its caked and screaming yellow bed,
and then, two yards away, the bloodied eyes
of his devilish self-portrait—

but I pause, instead, in your honor
(wanting to think only of the you you were)
before *Sunday Afternoon at the Grande Jatte*:
those bourgeois ghosts so primly posed

beside a silent stream,
                            and I think
how easily I see clear through them,
they're only shadows

with portentous dogs and bustles
whispering across a phantom light
that rises like swamp fever
from the Grand Jatte's golden ground. . . .

My dear one, my other self, you lay
bleeding to death
in a white chaos where they wouldn't
let us see you: tubes and clicking things,

fearful voices of the Code Team—
trache, pacemaker, tranfusions—
and what brilliance of the past
leaped from the ghastly tiles (did any?)

to recall you to the shadow
life on the Grande Jatte,
how we and Seurat studied for it,
sketching the couple over and over, their

arm-in-arm silence, their odd
placidity, and the trembling
radiance that blurred behind them
as they stood themselves, unconscious,

in an eerie shade a whole lot
scarier than Van Gogh's scream.

May 3, 1992: On the Surface

it's yellow-green, yellow and green
and blue and warm,

and the outlook
for tomorrow is the same:

rhododendrons blooming purple, oleanders
on the freeways, people

strolling on Solano
and people drinking beer

on decks and in cafés
here and there

on Telegraph or Shattuck, and people
rioting, yes darling, in L.A.,

as though this were 1789 or something,
and the president's complaining

although on the surface
it's still

quite still and mild with a smell
of orange blossom rising

(pittosporum said the botanist
I met last week)

and there's the anthropologist who also
wrote to me last week, he says

it's hot in Jersey too plus
evil's in our genes, he's

sure of it, there was a talk on this
(his book was central) at the Smithsonian

and I thought him cute
though rather short

but on the surface, here,
it's getting, every day,

a little bluer,
hotter—earthquake weather, some would say—

but on the surface, certainly,
the oaks are pollinating, sexual and yellow,

yellow-green,
and the kids are fine, too, really,

even if down there this new
warmth hasn't trickled through

to you
and it's so dull, I know,

and I suspect
nothing touches what's inside the silent

boxes, nothing creeps into the heaviness
that covers all of you

except the bulbs, the dreadful bulbs exploding
everywhere and rising

toward the surface
through this season's placid grass.

June 15, 1992: Widow's Walk, Harpswell, Maine

A moon like a bloody animal eye over the inlet,
low, low toward the hill as if struggling
to cool itself in the chill black salt of the mudflats;
and the salt stench of the marshes simmers around
the tipsy wharf I walk on.

                    My dear,
I ate what I was told to try—
tonight chowder, lobster, sweet corn
and a blueberry muffin; last night clams
and lobster, steamed, baked, stewed.

Yesterday Joanne and I wandered through Bath,
admiring the white and black whalers' mansions,
the widow's walks where stoic wives
paced with straining eyes, scanning the long
flat sea for specks of motion.

And I sucked in the light flung out by the sea
at Popham Beach, drank up the buckets of salt wind
shifting the pale New England sands.
I'm stuffed with this state where we summered
thirty years ago.

                Remember
the cabin on Frenchman's Bay,
swelled with our secret heat, under the covers,
while bats flapped through the pines
and moths banged on the screens?

That's how I feel:
                    bloated with love
too heavy to hold, fat as the past.
The wharf rocks with the weight
of what I carry—

                    myself and you,
too much for one scared woman,
yet I'm looking for more,
pacing and looking,
as if any minute now,

in the lingering blue of almost solstice,
the old tour boat might sputter up to me,
me and you at the rails,
squinting against the sun
and eager for souvenirs.

September 10, 1992:
Picking Wildflowers in New Hampshire

Wading through the meadow, a Keatsian
cloud of "small gnats swarming" round me,
a continuo of crickets underfoot,
I choose these few sparse blossoms
for my desk and in your memory.

You'd love, I know, the cottage in the pines
where this month I moon my days away, half-napping,
half-scribbling half-formed tales of you
and me and how you lived and why
you died,

        and love, I think, the sudden
furtive spears of goldenrod just thrusting up
along the winding road that rims this field,
the dense coarse grass I'm walking on, the line
of evergreens that walls each space I move in.

You'd love! I hate the phrase, I hate that bleak
subjunctive, never ending, always postulating
the impossible.
        What *would* you love, what *can* I love,
in the empty meadow, the unpeopled house?

And yet my grammer acquiesces, helpless.
Here's what you'd say, I tell myself.
You'd say:
        Look at these nameless wildflowers,
their skinny stems as tough as rubber bands,

their tiny leaves and petals opened just enough,
enough to suit their needs and the needs
of the DNA.
>They're economical,
they live on almost nothing.

If you have to, so can you.

November 26, 1992: Thanksgiving at the Sea Ranch, Contemplating Metempsychosis

You tried coming back as a spider.
I was too fast for you. As you
climbed my ankle, I swept you off, I ground you

to powder under my winter boot.
Shall I cherish the black widow,
I asked, because he is you?

You were cunning: you became
the young, the darkly masked
raccoon that haunts my deck.

Each night for weeks you tiptoed
toward the sliding doors, your paws
imploring, eyes aglow. *Let me in,*

Let me back in, you hissed,
swaying beside the tubbed fuchsia,
shadowing the fancy cabbage in its Aztec pot.

And you've been creatures of the air and sea,
the hawk that sees into my skull, the seal that barks
a few yards from the picnic on the shore.

Today you chose a different life, today
you're trying to stumble
through the tons of dirt that hold you down:

you're a little grove of mushrooms,
rising from the forest floor you loved.
Bob saw you in the windbreak—

November mushrooms, he said,
off-white and probably poisonous.
Shall I slice you for the feast?

If I eat you will I die back into your arms?
Shall I give thanks for God's wonders
because they all are you, and you are them?

The meadow's silent, its dead grasses
ignore each other and the evening walkers
who trample them. What will you be,

I wonder, when the night wind rises?
Come back as yourself, in your blue parka,
your plaid flannel shirt with the missing button.

These fields that hum and churn with life
are empty. There is nowhere
you are not, nowhere

you are not not.

from **Water Music**

5. *Hard Water*

stifling the pipes,
and that blue mean
taste on the tongue,

tang of the difficult
elements, each
asserting its own

will to endure, to be
known: keen
thin iron

in the mouth—and swallowed
filling the innocent
back of the throat,

the gullet that only wants
air and sweet and milky
in tender sips.

So hard you find its white
shadow in the tub,
a film of stone

grown in the hollow
where you were dumb enough
to let your body lie.

A film, a stain.
And veil on veil, the foreign
molecules insist on

clinging to their place.
Your place.
Every night when you rise

shiny from the bath,
your softness chilling
as comfort spills and pools

on the cold floor,
you try to scrub that
stain away.

Every morning the film
has thickened, where
all night the tap

dripped and toppled its hard
water into the same
roughening spot.

6. Brine

Instead of sweet or neutral,
instead of leafy,
instead of air,
instead of the long stream of light,
instead of the quick stitches of wind
fastening and loosening warmth,

the great wave comes over,
the mouth of bitterness opens,
the muscles of the deep
gut of salt
clench, the belly
of cold distends,

and you are taken in,
into the cave where
salt and bitter
are needles piercing your skin,
tiny knives writing their names
in every cell.

On some shore, some
mythical solid,
the water that falls
falls like the sort of goodness
Plato propounded—
and others are watching you there,

they believe in the blades of change,
they preach the archaic
doctrine of brine as womb,
while you spin through
the blistering gray
that spins through your eyes.

Hold your breath.
Don't tell them
the truth of the brine.
Be dull, be dumb.
Pretend you're a stone
in a kindly pond.

Don't ever let yourself name
the bitter that prints its name
in your blood.
Don't even let yourself taste
the buds of salt
that are tasting you.

7. The Water Table

It rises in darkness, indifferent,
rotting the dead and complicating roots.

It doesn't know it's there.
It doesn't know it is.

It knows it wants to spread,
to be level, to be everywhere.

It wants to enter everything,
it wants what happens to happen,

wants to be drawn upward,
to be lifted past the thick, the black,

into sheets of light,
to glitter in that light,

to devour the light
and sink again

into its own flatness,
its imperviousness.

And you—
you think you dine at the table of water

as shooting stars dine on the universe.

8. The Lake

is said to be the deepest in Europe.
Beyond Milan, the granite carbuncles,

the vast stiff lace they call the Duomo,
it goes greenly blackly down,

the cold inside it traveling as low
as the Swiss Diavolezza reaches high.

The twitch of minnows near the gravelly shore,
the punctuating snakes,

refuse to fall that far, where
flaccid dark meets muscle of ice.

Is it China, as the children think?
Is it a mind that has no bottom?

It is the opposite of all we believe.
It is the other side of the shriek of a bird or the scream of a cat.

The blank massifs stare into it.
Although Pliny and Serbelloni have come and gone

and these (the brooding walker says) remain,
they too will sag, draggle—

caduta massi!—
and erode into the viscous fluid

where groaning ferries float
like tiny cakes of light,

offering themselves to the dead.

9. Rain

In the night,
an immense seething through the trees,
a seething and hissing as of a hasty invasion
led by brilliant insects from the north,

and then a scratching a tearing
a sudden scarification of windows, a plunge
of something swift and shapeless
and impartial

into leaves dirt stones shells flesh,
a flashing without color
into color. . . .
In the kitchen garden

the shriveled petals of the pelargonium
tremble and are smashed,
the roots of carrots, cabbages,
dilate and reach and suck and rot.

And you who nod beside the reading lamp,
seeing in a drowned half-sleep
only the pink of your fingers
as they cling to the edges of this page,

have you heard that seething from the sky?
By the time you wake,
shake yourself,
and rise to close the blinds,

it is over and it is calm, calm
and over.

Spring Equinox, 1993: Puerto Vallarta, Playa de los Muertos

Nearer and nearer the Equator, nearer
the tropic of impossibles where
leaves don't die and blossoms

the size of paradise
open celestial jaws and on
the *playa de los muertos*

the dead are bathing, complacent,
in a sun of every color, they are
bathing in our memory of them:

they've forgotten to fear
their death, they've long forgotten
to fear their lives, and now

they bask, they almost smile, they
wait. Now and then
one remembers the reason—

the *wish*, the *walk*, the *swim*:
but it's hard to walk without
the drag of the body, to swim

without the flesh that rises on the curve
of every wave, hard to wish
without blood or nerve.

                    That's why
they need us, *you* need *me*:
to walk, to wish.

You don't know, I guess, but now,
right now, I'm watching you,
watching as you strive to rise,

watching as you stumble
to the rim of salt, the waterline.
And you see, my love

walks you across the border,
urges the wish, teaches the swim.
Camped on my own hot shore,

I send you forth—you deeply burning
in yourself like a floating candle,
you musing and lit with your own past—

I send you like a hieroglyph or a letter
to God, across the shining gulf,
toward the unimaginable ice cliffs

south of the south.

Calla Lilies

Stacked in banks of cream, pale foreigners,
they crane their long green necks, green bodies,
over irises, wild grasses, poppies,
calm and only mildly startled
by the light that quakes across the sky.

Down there, in the *before,*
everything was closed: what moved
moved inside the seals, the fastenings,
the enormous heaviness through which
from time to time
small stirrings crept.

                          But then the stones
softened, the gates of the cold unlocked.
Something began to lift them, something began
a steep crawl up the slope of shadow.

Now, bland and open in their bridal satin,
they extrude gold tongues, gold phalluses
into a warmth that loves them back,
and sway and bow in the Easter breeze.

Imperturbable as cream,
they have forgotten the wrists and ribs of the dead
from whose pallets they have risen.

February 11, 1994: Berkeley,
Anniversary Waltz Again

The year revolves toward pink and red,
toward the tiny Valentine
hearts of the plums,

each blossom a pink frill
and a core of blood, a frill
and its bloody core. . . .

Three times the nurses wheeled you into the icy room,
three-quarters of your life just barely over.
Three years since you set out for nowhere,

three years I've studied these blossoms alone,
the indifferent flush, the roseate
aplomb they set against bare blue.

To have gone on becoming without you!
Three nights now since we met in sleep,
and I told you sorrowfully

that you were dead—
three nights since you wept in rage,
lifted your handsome shadowy head and howled.

But how your face has changed!
You're beardless and pale,
a different man, a *spirit* man,

as if when we were spun away from each other,
as if when I took my first three giant steps
into another somewhere,

you too could never be the same,
you too had to go on becoming
and becoming other,

becoming alone. . . .
As if the only February thing
that's sure to be the same

is still the plum tree's
blind pink three-week waltz
with air and light and darkness.

VI

From *Blood Pressure* (1988)

from The Love Sequence

You Discover You're in Love with the Dead Prince

You thought, He must be pale, he must be silent,
he must sit by the river all morning gazing at nothing.
And when he sat on the bank, his eyes focused on nothing,
you thought, It's me he sees in the middle distance,
he's watching my dance, he's in love
with the dance of my invisible bones.

For him you turned your skin to cream.
You thought, he'll sip my body like a spirit
potion, and come to the secret
place of my heart—for he's the one
who loves my eyelids, he's the one
who bathes his wrist in the cold stream
because he dreams of the blue vein behind my ankle.

And all the time he was dead, he was the boy king
in the coffin of ice, the one with the mirror splinter
caught in his left eye, the royal child
attended by women and mourners,
whose long trance was demanded, they said, by mystic
signs from the stars.

                    In his dead cellar,
among the jewels and mirrors,
the sacred nurses feed him cream through tubes,
they bathe his silence in sweet wine.
All night a fire of thorny twigs
flickers cold, cold. . . .

You looked into the pale flames. You watched
the ceremonies of shadow. You wept.
You said you couldn't believe it.
You said, O prince, O friend, O lover,
climb out of that snowdrift
and come to this meadow where the blackberries ripen
and the bees hum like summer.

And he smiled in his trance, and said,
What snowdrift? What meadow? What summer?

How You Fell

You were the proud one, the kid in the secret room
lit by organdy curtains white as milk,
the one who had a special destiny
inscribed on her forehead with invisible ink.

April evenings sparrows lined up on your fire escape
to tell you their tales of old verandahs,
palm trees, Florida afternoons:
you were going to walk on warm sands, marry

the master of the plantation, command
the fountain that gushed wine.
Love would rain on you like geranium balm, love
would fortify your heart against everyone

except the one who was just, the one who loved you
more than his own bones, the one
whose beard shone in the wind
like the wild grass behind the schoolyard.

Who took you to the door of the oven?
Who walked you into the cooking pot? Who
introduced you to the vizier of silence with his
wand of ice, his cape of dead leaves?

You knew he'd enlisted under a blank banner, knew
he was missing crucial fingers, knew
he was the agent for somebody else.
But it didn't matter, you stayed put,

you baked in the cave of change,
your hair dampened, your
secret organs hummed with love.
When you came out,

he turned toward you, his pale gaze fell on you
like the headlights of a dark car
rounding a bend on an empty road at midnight.

He told you how little you mattered.

Behind him you heard the sea
falling and falling on terrible rocks.

You were sticky and thick with love
like the broken windowpane the witch painted over with sugar.

You Meet the Real Dream Mother-in-Law

In the anteroom of silence you waited to meet
the dream mother-in-law,
fingering old magazines, their exhausted edges, the places
where recipes were torn away. . . .

You sat straight as a washboard in your
naugahyde chair, holding your breath,
never complaining: you knew
she was in there and how it would be—

the long still room with blood-colored rugs,
the tables on eighteenth-century stilts, the hair
Atlantic gray, the bone china cups
with blue frost, the silver-tipped cane, the misty

voice of Ethel Barrymore, saying,
I've waited so long, *he's* waited so long,
but how glad we are, my dear,
that you're the one!

And then the talk would unfold like fine lace,
the talk of women who'd take a lifetime
to trace this intricate design. . . .
Silk the color of tea leaves, fingers keen as crystal,

she'd love your sonnets, give you
sherry that had slept in the cabinet
since her impudent sister ran off with that
mean metaphysician: she'd

want you to have her grandmother's sapphire,
tell you legends of sombre attics,
clasp your hand between ivory gloves
and make you hers, hers. . . .

When they opened the double doors and led you in,
you were surprised to find a naked waitress
sulking on a shell-shaped sofa.

Her son winked and blew poison darts at you
like the bad kid next door, the one
who was always stoned on something rotten.

She accused you of doing wicked things in the dark,
told you to hurry up and start sorting grain, said
you should remember there was a mountain you'd have to climb.

You stared like a fool at her granite breasts, her great
snowy belly, her whole
ferocious body.

       Smoke
curled from between her thighs
like the awful breath of factories.

The One He Loves

She's the figure skater you've always hated,
the princess of the spelling bee, the ice queen
in velvet and fur
with muscles tough as tusks
and hair the color of charm bracelets.

Next to her you're flabby and noisy, something
made of jelly instead of sinew,
something that shivers and whimpers
and passes out in the dark, a princess of pain
with weak ankles and a head full of misspelled sentences.

Once you asked her the secret: how do you
always keep your skates on, how do you memorize
the whole dictionary? She smiled and talked too slowly,
a native telling a foreigner
the way through some inexplicable city.

In the palace of his mind
they reign forever on twin frost thrones.
Suave servants in black and white
circle them like gulls, offering trays
on which odd canapés swarm thick as wishes.

She nibbles, royal, muscular, silent.
He watches, a furtive cat on the edge of shadow:
he wants her to burn his skin, wants her
to crack his bones, wants the fine spray from her skates
to baptize his wrists like radioactive sleet.

Around them expensive dancers loop and spin.
She and he yawn, hum, play chess, play Scrabble.
A cold flame flickers between them
on polished granite; only they
know what it means, only they.

The Love Sickness

You lie on the sofa all day, washed in fog,
your heart twittering like a thrush among prickly branches.
You think you're that last black tree before the beach, the one
that trembles so close to the cliff edge it seems to have
one toe in the abyss. . . .

Your toes are dissolving like that, your whole body
melting and thinning, becoming transparent, becoming
the room, the sofa, the fog, the twittering inside.

It's the love sickness! It's the damned old nausea
of desire, the ague that shakes the last right angle
of reason from your bones
and turns the world to stupid
metaphors for passion.

You peer through the fog like a nearsighted hiker
on a stony seaside path.
Your toes and knees are gone, and the rest of you
dissolving fast: soon you'll be nothing
but the buzz of love, the ache, the fever.

And now, out there, where a window once was,
you think you see the face of the one you love!
It shines toward you like a tiny moon
on a misty night, or a lucky penny,
or a pale expensive sugar candy.

The Last Poem about the Snow Queen

> *Then it was that little Gerda walked into the Palace, through the*
> *great gates, in a biting wind. . . . She saw Kay, and knew him at*
> *once; she flung her arms round his neck, held him fast, and cried,*
> *"Kay, little Kay, have I found you at last?"*
> *But he sat still, rigid and cold.*
>   —Hans Christian Anderson, "The Snow Queen"

You wanted to know "love" in all its habitats, wanted
to catalog the joints, the parts, the motions, wanted
to be a scientist of romance: you said
you had to study everything, go everywhere,
even here, even
this ice palace in the far north.

You said you were ready, you'd be careful.
Smart girl, you wore two cardigans, a turtleneck,
furlined boots, scarves,
a stocking cap with jinglebells.
And over the ice you came, gay as Santa,
singing and bringing gifts.

Ah, but the journey was long, so much longer
than you'd expected, and the air so thin,
the sky so high and black.
What are these cold needles, what are these shafts of ice,
you wondered on the fourteenth day.
What are those tracks that glitter overhead?

The one you came to see was silent,
he wouldn't say "stars" or "snow,"
wouldn't point south, wouldn't teach survival.
And you'd lost your boots, your furs,
now you were barefoot on the ice floes, fingers blue,
tears freezing and fusing your eyelids.

Now you know: this is the place
where water insists on being ice,
where wind insists on breathlessness,
where the will of the cold is so strong
that even the stone's desire for heat
is driven into the eye of night.

What will you do now, little Gerda?
Kay and the Snow Queen are one, they're a single
pillar of ice, a throne of silence—
and they love you
the way the teeth of winter
love the last red shred of November.

A Year Later

A year later you wonder how you ever loved him.
After all, you tell yourself, he was never more
than a frog, not even pretending to be a prince.
Even then, you think, even in those convulsions of love,
you saw the warts,
the leafslick spots, the cloak of slime:

he was silent because he couldn't speak,
motionless because he couldn't walk.
And yes, you knew it! Yes!
You only loved your own love, only
feasted on your own heart, only cherished
your own fondness for frogs.

But even as you rock and reprimand,
rock and groan, eyes shut in shame,
you remember the forest clearing,
the mossy lip of the well, the way the black water
fell to the center of the stone world,
a shaft of ice that split the grass,

and then there were ripples, circles,
animal honkings—*rivet, rivet*—
and your frog leaped out of silence.
As you sprawled on the lumpy ground, your own
reflection grew in the pool
where he rode like a toy boat.

You bent to kiss the water near him,
wanting to enter his cold glisten,
wanting to seize and wear him like a brooch,
wanting to swallow him as if he were a measure
of some bitter, alien liqueur.
Down and down you bent,

toward the emerald skin, the golden eyes,
closer than ever before
to your own wavering face.

The Return of the Muse

You always knew you wrote for him, you said
He is the father of my art, the one who watches all night,
chain-smoking, never smiling, never satisfied.
You liked him because he was carved from glaciers,
because you had to give him strong wine to make him human,
because he flushed once, like a November sunset,
when you pleased him.

But you didn't love him.
You thought that was part of the bargain.
He'd always be there like a blood relative,
a taciturn uncle or cousin,
if you didn't love him. You'd hand him poems,
he'd inspect them, smoke, sip, a business deal,
and that would be that.

Then he went away and you hardly noticed.
Except you were happy, you danced on the lawn,
swelled like a melon, lay naked long mornings,
brushed your hair more than you needed.
Your breasts grew pink and silky,
you hummed, you sucked the pulp of oranges, you forgot
all about words.

                    And when you were
absolutely ignorant,
                    he came back,
his jacket of ice flashed white light,
his cap of pallor bent toward you, genteel, unsmiling.
He lit a cigarette, crossed his legs,
told you how clumsy you were.

Ah, then, love seized you like a cramp,
you doubled over in the twist of love.
You shrieked. You gave birth to enormous poems.

He looked embarrassed and said how bad they were.
They became beasts, they grew fangs and beards.
You sent them against him like an army.

He said they were all right
but added that he found you, personally,
unattractive.

      You howled with love,
you spun like a dervish with rage, you
kept on writing.

Accident

Something rushes out of the black broth
at the other end of the road, a red needle,
sirens weeping, splotches of light

punching holes in silence.
We slow to a clumsy procession
and shamble hood to hull

past the theater of blood on the dirt shoulder
where pale curved shapes arrange themselves
above flat black ones.

Stretchers, broken glass, a bashed VW—
if we could all get out and tiptoe past
we all would:

I feel the old wound in my eyelid
opening again, the slit
that lets in darkness

and shows me how it took an hour for forty cars
to press the dead deer on yesterday's road
into a dull mat,

the slit of vision
keen as a splinter that goes in and in
and still more deeply in.

Blood Pressure

The white-sleeved woman wraps a rubber
sleeve around your arm, steps back, listens,
whistles.

      How it pounds in you, how it
urges through you, how it asserts
its power like a tide of electrons

flashing through your veins, shocking your fingertips,
exhausting the iron gates of your heart.
Alive, always alive, it hisses,

crackling like the lightning snake that splits
the sky at evening, *alive,* a black rain
lashing the hollows of your body,

alive, alive.
      You sit quietly on the cold table,
the good boy grown up into

the good man. You say
you want nothing, you'll diet, you
won't complain. Anyway, you say,

you dream of January weather,
hushed and white, the cries of light
silenced by a shield of ice.

Behind your eyes, something
like a serpent moves, an acid tongue
flicking at your cheekbones, something
voracious, whipping your whole body
hard: you're sad, you flush a
dangerous pink, you tell her

you can't understand the fierce rain
inside you, you've always hated that awful
crackling in your veins.

In the Golden Sala

Sun of Sicilian hillsides,
heat of poppies opening like fierce
boutonnières of Apollo,
light of Agrigento, fretting the sea and the seaside cliffs—
light of the golden *sala*,
the great *sala* of the ruined *palazzo*
where my Sicilian grandmother and her nine children
camped outside Palermo.

Gold leaf, gold moldings,
shredding tapestries with gold threads.
"Once it belonged to a prince.
Mama kept chickens on the terrace
but they came in sometimes, and the donkey too."
Gold chairs, gilt around the windows,
angels with shining hair and empty eyes
staring from the ceiling.

"Mama made our beds in the corners:
the big room scared us, we thought
the prince's ghost was there."
Gold railings where her laundry hung,
gold curtains, new eggs under them.
Her cooking fire in a corner,
the center of the *sala* a cave of gold
for spankings and scoldings.

"Mama was a midwife, knew
everything about herbs and births.
The peasant women came from farms around Palermo
so she could help them."
On floors still streaked with gold
she made them spaces
in the dazzling spaces where the prince once walked.
Gold of forgotten dances, tattered rugs.

When a new baby slid out in a splash of water
he must have looked up, dazed,
toward the prince's Apollonian light,
and the black eyes of the midwife
and the black eyes of the midwife's nine black-haired children
would have looked quizzically down,
as if from a high cliff by the sea
hot and yellow with new poppies.

Grandpa

Garlic and cigars recall you, stuffed mushrooms,
spinach ravioli, Genoa haunting your kitchen,

and you with your dragging foot—
bad circulation, maybe a stroke—

5'3", bald, gray forehead, gray mustache, failed
restaurateur, failed painter, thinning as you cooked,

thinning to the one you were in the bottle-green
Hotel Negresco uniform in Nice,

only now in Queens, pining for the old farm,
the hills above the sea. . . .

When they paced the cobbled wharf at Genoa
planning their moves five centuries ago,

what did they imagine? The men
must have been seamen: leaning landward like old walls,

they must have dreamed you as a wave
breaking on some far island. You must

have been their intention for the future. When the great
ship set sail, heeling and running free,

you lay in the hold, naked of uniforms,
painter of frescoes, master of promised spices,

rosy, perfect. What accident
of the mid-Atlantic

turned you into a scrap of cargo
lost by the civilization of the wind—

the calm sea, the prosperous voyage—
that left you and your dragging foot behind?

My Grandmother in Paris

Paris. 1900. A sky of corrugated iron. Snow and mud.
Beggars like heaps of debris on street corners.
Women with pink cheeks melting in doorways.
Splashes of laughter, church bells, creaking boots.
Puccini's Paris, Paris of *La Bohème*, Paris
of garrets and prisons, Paris of sweet fevers, Paris

of phlegm and sweat, ivory breasts, skylights, *opéra*:
Paris of Wagner and Rilke, Paris of delicious
nineteenth-century melancholy, Paris where streetlights
glisten through the winter twilight
like pomegranates in hell.
                              Twilight.

My grandmother walks in the Bois de Boulogne
under frosted chestnuts. She's twelve years old,
a round-faced girl just come from Russia,
her hair in skinny braids
like strange embroidery around her head.
She's on her way to the house of the Russian priest

where her mother cooks and cleans
but she watches, wondering, as carriages plunge
through the slush of the Bois, their lamps
leaping like goblin heads, their blanketed horses
clopping docile as cows through all the Paris noise.
Baudelaire is dead, Rimbaud dead in Africa, Gertrude Stein

thinking in Baltimore, Picasso painting in Barcelona.
My grandmother has learned three words of French:
allo, comment, combien. Amedée, the boy she's
going to marry four years from now
is in Nice with his sister Eugénie,
who will die next year at nineteen,

and his sister Rosette, who will die at forty.
My grandmother is still tired from last week.
She stops to sit on a low wall beside the road
and begins to shape a tiny angel out of crumbs of snow.
From a passing *fiacre* a young clerk off to the *opéra*
sees her round pink face suspended like a small balloon

in the blue air.
                         What is she thinking
as she pats a cold celestial head and frozen wings?
Is she remembering the awful train ride
across Europe, the bonfires at the Polish border, the shouts
as the engine chuffed into Berlin? No. She rises,

makes her angel into a snowball and tosses it at a tree.
She's thinking of Russia, of her grandmother back in the room
in Rostov-on-the-Don, of the ice like silver on the river
all winter and long into spring, of the black fields
outside town and the old stories of Baba Yaga and the tales
she has also heard of the red-haired cossack

said to be her own father.

                            She walks faster.
It's late and cold. Her mother will worry.
The fat priest will be cross. Paris
grows around her like an enigmatic alphabet.
Even the trees are different here. No firs, no birches!

As she walks, Baba Yaga's house on chicken legs
steps delicately away across snowy meadows
and her father the cossack, with his furry animal head, fierce teeth,
                            red beard,
gallops into glacial distances.
(Does she suspect that from now on
she'll never really know any language again?)

Tomorrow the priest will be sixty. To celebrate
he'll buy a Swiss cane at the Galéries Lafayette.

                            In seventy years
my grandmother will twirl that cane and dance a two-step
among the eucalyptuses above San Francisco Bay,
singing me the song about the lost princess of the Volga

while, far below, the cold Pacific
glitters like an ice field.

Anniversary Waltz

—for E.

Talking to you is as embarrassing as talking
to myself: I think everyone will stare, they'll say
Look at that crazy lady, muttering
Love, Love, like a lunatic!

We stoop together in the garden,
stuck in gummy cabbage patches,
nagging, laughing, cursing. When you look up,
I admire your eyebrows, as always.

Satanic, magisterial, Jewish!
I used to dream myself to sleep picturing your eyebrows
raised in my direction!
Yet soon enough we moved into a German ballroom

with bamboo partitions.
You wrote your famous letter to the I.G.
Senators wrote to us.
Our firstborn baby died.

Twenty-one years went by.
More children, more kitchens, better partitions.
Typewriters, studies, weeping in the pantry.
Making love like adolescents on the sly.

Your beard begins to get gray,
but not your eyebrows.
We're stuck in the thick of it, we smile wryly,
we fatten, we grow dumb.

Once in a while
I have to hang on to your hand.
I cannot imagine who else
we might have become.

Ponce de León

—*for E.*

In Hallandale and Hollywood
the seventy-year-old Jewish ladies
and their shrunken sneakered husbands

are hurrying out for the Early Bird Specials:
bent, red-haired Emma R., two
sandwiches at a time,

hops to at the Little Rascal,
Yan ladles wontons, Rico flings veal.
The skinny old men eat voraciously,

they eat as though sandwiches and wontons
would keep them alive forever, alive and on the beach,
where I want you to be, you, fifty-three-years-old

now, with your rosy lips and graying beard.
Well, why, when I think of you, do I
think of islands in swamps, Ponce de León places

where your eyes would always glitter?
Let's go back to the early world of the sword grass,
away from the Rascals,

back to the heaving world where the rare blue heron
meditates above water hyacinth
and the marsh hen skids in

for a splashy landing:
it gets dark there at six,
after a flush of rose like yours,

and we'll sleep on a bank like two
bad alligators, two stones.
The fishermen will steer toward us, flashlights

glinting, then turn back:
Don't disturb the Seminoles.
These are the old people,

the ones who were here when
the buzzards first took flight
and the world began.

2085

It's 2085, you're walking on a dirt road
in Sicily, you're my blood-
kin, a seventeen-year-old girl

with black curls and a faint smudge of
shadow on your upper lip.
                              Have you

come from New York to find lost ancestors,
or have you always been here?
Dry hills, stacks of heat,

tower around you; nearby, there are goats, donkeys, chickens,
a smell of dung simmering,
and smoke, grain, *rosmarino;*

in the sky, a track of supersonic light—
but you don't look up, you're reading, thinking,
trying to imagine the past,

and my sentences won't help you, though they
brood in you like chromosomes:
                              I can't

tell you who I was, in my queer costume,
with my modern ideas.
                              My words

stand in the fields beside you—
stones, dead trees—the way
the land you walk through

stood behind me, an unknown monument.
And now the road unfolds and shines ahead
like the history neither of us understands.

It turns you
toward the sea, toward
the inarticulate Aegean.

VII

From *Emily's Bread* (1984)

For the Muses

They said I couldn't find you.
They said because I'm a *she*,
because the *s* in my name blurs my features,
a hiss around my face like uncombed hair,
you wouldn't be interested.

They said my breasts would hinder me,
heavy, hard to carry, with nipples like blinded eyes.
They said the inflatable rubber cell in my belly
would frighten you, and the lips between my legs:
you'd expect me to eat you up!

But I remember you too well.
You were the immigrant aunts I visited
in the suburbs of my childhood,
keeping house with what you'd salvaged
on the long flight from Paris:

diamonds in the linings of your coats,
embroideries from the 1890s,
Egyptian jewelry, a samovar, old
cashmere scarves, a rosewood wardrobe
larger than the bathroom.

Aunt Rose, your hair was black, it grew in wings from your
     forehead.
Aunt Lil, your hair was white, it circled your skull like a shawl.
You see, I remember.
And your fourth-floor flat, where I visited you, where you
fed me oranges and honey, cakes and wine—

I remember that too: the print
of the lovers in the forest, the witch
pictures on the walls, the plants
that hummed in the dark, the
black feet of the peacock.

You spoke to me there, you told me the stories.
I was yours as much as any boy.
Or more: for the notion of my breasts was yours,
you planned them, you designed them.
And the afternoon you led me to the rosewood wardrobe

and opened the great carved door
you smiled when I myself pulled out the center drawer,
smiled when all that light came spilling out
and wrapped itself around my arms, my thighs, my shoulders
like a bolt of old satin.

"A mantle, not a shroud," you said.

The Dressmaker's Dummy

In my grandmother's room, treasures of old mahogany,
intricate and enigmatic as the 1890s:
the three-paned mirror, the great highboy
with knobs like cabbage roses and expensive brasses,

the bed of generations—brown and black, teak and rosewood,
    inlays
older than I could ever be—and a mattress
soft from half a century of sleepers,
and quilts, and goose feathers,

and cast adrift on the crimson carpet
a dressmaker's dummy, headless, armless,
a barren stork on one steel leg. . . .
The stork that brought me—for as I grew it grew with me,

its plaster hips were padded to mimic mine,
and when I sprouted breasts so did the dummy,
and as I lengthened it slid up its pole, became lean, became
    bone,
became my own self, hardening, final,

and at night, through the shadows, I watched it shine
in the mirror, the streetlamps casting white eyes
on its ludicrous height, white scorn on its hips,
its empty neck, its stiff stuck frame:

and still it's there in my grandmother's room,
curved like the prow of a ship, cleaving the air
dumb as a wooden whaler's wife, a hopeless
image of me, frozen and bare,

sailing forward into the triple mirror,
wading waist-deep, a dead lady, into the future.

On the Third Hand

On the one hand
I am afraid. I wear a school ring.
I prick my tender fingers, remember typewriters,
        carry hammers.

On the other hand
I believe there's nothing to fear.
I wear a wedding ring. I have pink fingernails.
        My skin is soft as vanilla cream.

On the third hand
I wear the rings of crystal and pollen
and the rings the Etruscans fashioned
from feathers, auguries, seeds, and
        salts of strange origin:

these rings murmur in the dark,
murmur and click in foreign tongues,
keeping my cold third hand awake,
promising pleasures unique as fingerprints,
pains closer to bone than skin.

The fingers of my third hand are green,
they are yellow and green.
Someone gave them to me in a dream
when I was twenty-nine.

With the third hand
I write letters to the world of glass,
letters instantly read and memorized
by missionaries of the light, letters swallowed
by emptiness, letters conveyed by silent messengers
to polar silences. (Somewhere
in other words, they are well known.)

On the third hand
I play the piano of grass, and looped around cold fingers
I carry the green keys that unlock the door in the oak
behind which my great aunts live smiling
in a parlor lined with glittering samovars:

with the third hand
I turn all the handles, and once again
the ancient tea steams out like rain.

Emily's Bread

1857 Emily's bread won a prize at the annual Cattle Show.
1858 Emily served as a judge in the Bread Division of the
      Cattle Show.
                    —John Malcolm Brinnin, "Chronology,"
                    Selected Poems of Emily Dickinson

Inside the prize-winning blue-ribbon loaf of bread,
there is Emily, dressed in white,
veiled in unspeakable words,
not yet writing letters to the world.

No, now she is the bride of yeast,
the wife of the dark of the oven,
the alchemist of flour, poetess of butter,
stirring like a new metaphor in every bubble

as the loaf begins to grow.
Prosaic magic, how it swells,
like life, expanding, browning
at the edges, hardening.

Emily picks up her pen, begins to scribble.
Who'll ever know? "This is my letter
to the world, that never. . . ."
Lavinia cracks an egg, polishes

the rising walls with light. Across
the hall the judges are making notes:
firmness, texture, size, flavor.
Emily scribbles, smiles. She knows it is

the white aroma of her baking skin
that makes the bread taste good.
Outside in the cattle pen the blue-ribbon heifers
bellow and squeal. Bread means nothing to them.

They want to lie in the egg-yellow sun.
They are tired of dry grain, tired of grooming and love.
They long to eat the green old meadow
where they used to live.

Daguerreotype: Governess

She comes toward us like a troublesome memory,
carrying her basket of *maybes*, her clergyman's umbrella,
her grandfather, her clergyman, her large gold watch
in the shape of a decaying apple.

Her eyes are darning needles, her breasts pincushions.
Between her thighs, icy as panes of glass,
a thin ribbon of silk flutters and cries.
There are no strong verbs in her sentences

because there is no skin on the back of her hands.
There is no end to her paragraphs
because her fingers are tipped with the shivering wings
of tiny insects—moths, beetles, stingless bees.

Four children are attached like yo-yos to her knees.
On her head she wears a feathered hat, dark as a beard.
She tells us she'd like to go back to the parsonage
with its kitchen of apples, its dim windows, its stony orchard.

She misses the hoops in the garden, she says, and the shells,
and the wise silence of the stuffed parrot.
If she cannot return, she explains, she would like to die.
If she cannot die, she will accept her life

as the most expedient solution.
Behind her we see the shape of a large trunk or bureau.
For some reason, it seems clear
she stores little vials of her mother's blood in there.

Daguerreotype: "Fallen" Woman

The clock between her thighs ticks like a heart of gold:
satins, furbelows, no matter what she wears
she knows it's there, quick treasure, time machine that carries her,
pink nymph of the *pavé*,
from mattress to mattress, day to day.

Rustling her colors, she tells us this
between gulps of beer,
confides, "It's the drink that gets me through,"
grins, twitches her skirt. Her hair
is a curious shade of green

(from spit and sweat, she thinks)
and clings like fingers to her neck;
her frayed shawl, dull as a night's work,
sways around her hips; her breasts are question marks.
Some afternoons she sleeps, she says, and dreams,

green ringlets in her eyes,
that she's a tree, falling through the Thames,
falling through the easy mud,
into Australia, where the sun is hot
and an armless man sucks out her hole, her clock, her heart.

Daguerreotype: Wet Nurse

Everything about her thick—thick wrists, thick ankles,
skin thick as felt—she dawdles
through the rich man's nursery,
stupid, staring at nothing, wearing her heavy body
idly as the heifer wears her bell.

When the silk-skinned child stirs and whimpers
in its slim mahogany stall,
she yawns, offers a nipple thick as cheese,
hot as the haystacks where she lies in dreams,
legs spread to country lovers.

Rocking and dozing, oozing juice, she says
she still remembers the other child,
the wailing one she left in the suburbs
to be weaned on tea or water.
It had, she thinks, red down

on its wobbly head; or was it brown?
She sleeps. The child sucks, gurgles,
also sleeps. Behind thick lids
we see her pupils flicker, back and forth.
A small vein pulses in her neck, while

from somewhere far inside her breast, her skull,
rises the humming of an insect self, thin, elegant,
spinning a web of bitter milk
to drown the mild
breathing of the rich man's child.

Bas Relief: Bacchante

She's not at all as we expected, wearing
(instead of oiled breasts, a torn toga, a sexy swoon)
a sort of fur ruff and the calm look
of those animal-headed judges, wise as roots,
who rule the world below.

They were the ones, she says, who watched when Orpheus,
that show-off, gave the look that kills
to Eurydice on the stony path.
Betrayed girl-bride, stuck halfway up the hill
and halfway down!

                  Her fur ruff twitches
as she makes this case. It's clear
she never liked the bastard anyway,
the swaggering bastard with his silver flute,
precious proboscis, mean baton,

commanding silence, silence from everyone,
shutting the trees up, quieting the wind
and the quick birds, and the women.
Without his manly anthems,
everything, she says, would sing, would sing.

As she speaks, a furry feathery humming
rises from the stones she stands on
and we see she's after all a lioness,
serenely hungry to dismember him.
But behind her, hidden among leaves,

dressed in a gauzy apron, a crinoline, a rhinestone necklace,
there is Isis, that apple blossom queen,
that silly sister-in-law,
that superintendent of nurses,
ready as ever to pick up the bloody pieces.

Sculpture: Naiad/Fountain

Stone faced, living always in water,
feeling always the pulse of water,
its dazzling thickness, shape, weight, power,

how is she to say the sentence
that curls like a fern around her lips?
Consider: at night, while you sleep on feathers,

she is still in the cold heartbeat,
the veils of clarity shifting before her eyes
like panes of ice, keen, murderous.

Legless, rooted to that blind center
where the water churns, murmurs, prepares
its terrifying leap upward,

she's forgotten the warm stream where she swam
that afternoon the sculptor captured her,
forgotten nipples and milk, fingertips and leaves,

and everything except the waiting, the white sound,
and the beat, the colorless engine beat
that explodes *over, around,* and again, *over, around,*

caging her in thinness,
in light that praises and denies,
in the gasping alien measure

of the sculptor's breath.
Do you wonder if she dreams of death?
Turning in your sleep, shut eyes moving in the dark,

do you imagine her return to the river of her girlhood,
where sun and shade shape the water
and she pioneers, shouting, to the current's mouth?

You wake and look: she's still here,
fixed in the blank piazza, which has
no words to ease the violence of her silence.

Elegy

The pages of history open. The dead enter.
It is winter in the spine of the book
where they land, inexplicable texts,
and a small rain falling, a mist of promises,
disjointed sentences, woes, failures.

The dead are puzzled:
was it for this they left
the land of grammar, the syntax of their skin?
We turn the pages. We read.
Sometimes, in moments of vertigo,

we notice that they're speaking.
Tiny whinings and murmurings arise,
as of insects urging their rights, their dissatisfactions,
invisible insects dwelling uncomfortably
in the margins, in the white spaces around words.

The Night Grandma Died

Adrift on the pillows. "She just died," said the nurse.
"A heart attack," the doctor said.
"It was easy, peaceful," I told her daughter.

I tried to picture the pincers of heaven
reaching down and twitching her, a little wrinkled diamond,
from the sweet white cot she lay on.

Tears and sniffles. My consolation
didn't work. Not even for me.
What was it, in the end, that wouldn't go away?

The bed. The feel of the cold rails
sliding up and down when people came with needles,
the gray rails grating, clanking, her fingers

yearning toward them like a baby's lips,
hoping for suction. And the white sheets
stiff as sails, scraping skin as if skin were wind, insubstantial.

And the night light, flashing, going out, flashing again.
And the tough mattress, sullen as a shark's back,
rising toward the nurse's hands

on its steel track.

Simplicity

—for Elliot

Wishing to praise
the simple, the univocal, the one
word that falls like a ripe fruit
into an infinite well,
I watch

that easy old couple, limber
sixty-year-olds,
strolling, maybe just finished jogging,
under the plum trees.
Over their mild

gray heads the air
is pink with blossoms
accomplishing themselves;
under their tan, accomplished Keds
the sidewalk's pink with petals.

She turns to him and speaks, a word
that fills and falls like another petal,
easy, simple:
a word of thirst?—*milk? wine?*—
a word of love?—*good run?*—

whatever,
it befalls him
light as the stroke of a branch,
clear as color,
and he nods, smiles.

I want to learn that word, I want
to hold that word under my tongue
like a sip of milk,
I want to inhale that word
the way that gray-haired woman, now,

turns back to the tree
and inhales the lucid perfume
of a blossom that promises
ripeness, night, the sweetness
of the plum.

Sitting

—for Carole Peel

I assume the pose,
ring finger to temple,
the thoughtful subject,
eyes on a mythic distance.

Knife-keen pencil, square of blank light,
you begin, stooping, squinting, rearranging
my arms and yours, explaining
"It's so physical, so—so—"

No word comes: you laugh, shake your head,
bend to the space that wants to be filled, while
Mozart swarms around us, a hive of life.
"Music helps—"

Beyond your window
sun clasps the green lines
of a redwood—"so physical"—
I want to reach and touch

but the pose becomes me, holds me,
my body aches and stiffens, now
I'm passing out of myself,
now I'm spreading under your fingers,

my eyes darkening on the rough
sheet, your quick strokes
making me more severe until I look up
wondering how you'll finish me

and see you're laughing, happy at how your pencil
cuts my mouth, just here
into a neat corner. . . .
Flat on the page, I stare, I stare.

Your ruffly white blouse, navy jeans,
black sneakers, yellow hair
strain through my sketchy
adjectives and nouns.

The Emily Dickinson Black Cake Walk

*1866: Ned . . . inherits his Uncle Emily's ardor for the lie. My flow-
ers are near and foreign, and I have but to cross the floor to stand in the
Spice Isles. . . .*

*1883: Your sweet beneficence of Bulbs I return as Flowers, with a bit
of the swarthy Cake baked only in Domingo. . . .*
                                        —*The Letters of Emily Dickinson*

Black cake, black night cake, black
thick cake out of which Emily
leaps in bubbles of bitter sweetness—
lucid or dark balloons of Emily,
Emilie, Uncle Emily,
Dickinson, Nobody—
black Emily Dickinson cake,

how does your sugar grow?
What is the garden, where
is the furrow, whose
are the pods of heat and shadow?
How did black bulbs dissolve their iron,
leaves their silence, bees their drone of sunset honey
into the oven that cooked you firm?

Black cake, black Uncle Emily cake,
I tunnel among your grains of darkness
fierce as a mouse: your riches
are all my purpose, your currants and death's eye raisins
wrinkling and thickening blackness,
and the single almond of light she buried
somewhere under layers of shadow. . . .

One day I too will be Uncle Sandra:
iambic and terse, I'll hobble the tough sidewalks,
the alleys that moan *go on, go on*.
O when I reach those late-night streets,
when acorns and twigs
litter my path like sentences
the oaks no longer choose to say,

I want that cake in my wallet.
I want to nibble as I hobble.
I want to smile and nibble
that infinite black cake,
                         and lean
on Uncle Emily's salt-white
ice-bright sugar cane.

VIII

The Summer Kitchen (1983)

The Summer Kitchen

In June when the Brooklyn garden
boiled with blossom,
when leaflets of basil lined the paths
and new green fruitless fingers of vine
climbed the airy arbor roof,

my Sicilian aunts withdrew
to the summer kitchen,
the white bare secret room
at the bottom of the house.
Outside, in the upper world,

sun blistered the bricks of the tiny
imitation Taormina terrace where fierce
socialisti uncles
chain-smoked Camels and plotted politics;
nieces and nephews tussled

among thorny blood-colored
American roses;
a pimply concrete
birdbath-fountain dribbled ineffectual
water warm as olive oil.

Cool and below it all,
my aunts labored among great cauldrons
in the spicy air
of the summer kitchen: in one kettle
tomatoes bloomed into sauce;

in another, ivory *pasta*
leaped and swam;
on the clean white table
at the center of the room
heads of lettuce flung themselves open,

and black-green poles of zucchini
fell into slices of yellow,
like fairy tale money.
Skidding around the white
sink in one corner

the trout that Uncle Christopher brought back
from the Adirondacks gave up
the glitter of its fins
to the glitter of *Zia* Francesca's
powerful knife.

Every August day *Zia* Petrina
rose at four to tend the morning:
smoky Greek chignon
drawn sleek,
she stood at the sink.

Her quick shears
flashed in the silence,
separating day from night, trunk
from branch, leaf
from shadow.

As the damp
New World sunrays struggled to rise
past sooty housetops,
she'd look suddenly up
with eyes black as the grapes

that fattened in the arbor:
through one dirt-streaked window
high above her
she could see the ledge of soil
where her pansies and geraniums anchored.

Higher still,
in tangles of heat,
my uncles' simmering garden grew,
like green steam swelling from the cool
root of her kitchen.

The Brussels Sprouts

splotch the hillside like dried
sea vegetables, green and yellow, stinking
of winter, smugglers of brine.
                               All night

they tiptoed inland, up from the dim
beach, past the hairy cliff edge, over
the black toe of the mountain
to this field.   Here

they must make their stand, here
hundreds of sprouts must swell
along hundreds of stiff
necks of silence.

I wander mystified among them.
They're going to seed,
my friend the gardener says.
Their heads are opening!

Opening, seeding:
the hillside is quiet as rocks.
A mile away the sea yearns inward,
plunges, sucks.

The sprouts yawn like arctic
cabbages, a damp tongue of salt
flickering
in the pit of each green throat.

Five Potatoes

Heavy and blind, swollen with themselves, five potatoes wobble on the drainboard near the sink. When I met them they were passionate: stitched into thick loam, they drove all their strength into a hundred eyes. Now they've lost their purpose. But anyway I'll peel them, boil them, slice them, feed my children their forgotten visions.

I hum a little under my breath as I scrub and scrape. *Changes*, I sing, *transformations!* The cold water from the tap foams over my fingers. Just now, in Africa, a !Kung grandmother rises, picks up her stick, slings her pack across her shoulder, and walks away from the cooking fire. She's going to ford the river at the narrow place where the trout jump and the leopard comes down to drink, going to travel up the muddy path along the bank in the buzzing early morning light, and dig for yams for her children in the wild field beyond the village.

Turnips

At first I thought they were marble spheres
inexplicably sprouting coarse green hairs.
I wondered who cracked them open,
how crumbs of soil slid into invisible clefts,
what seeds had to do to fasten roots
in such fierce rock.
                                    But then
I saw they were alive and fibrous,
stout pots of sap, sealed containers
of something I didn't understand.

Half in, half out of the ground
they gazed up at me
like a hundred white eyes, thoughtful
eyes with purple bruises, as if someone had
scooped out the blank eyeballs
of a museumful of giant classical statues. . . .

And perhaps they weren't looking up at all!
Perhaps they were staring down,
down into archaeological layers beneath them,
down past the traffic of roots and worms
to melancholy wells and graphite tunnels
only they could comprehend. . . .

I took three of the wisest home
and simmered them for supper.

How many women have eaten the salty sweet intelligence
of the Acropolis
with broth and butter, cream and nutmeg?

The Leeks

fatten like marsh weeds, silvery pipes
exhaling the mild onion smell
of Vermont April.

They tell me I want to be an American,
I want a name that ends in a Protestant consonant
instead of a Catholic vowel!

Stooping above the cool
New England fronds,
I become a red-haired freckled

Presbyterian girl: I've inherited
a farmhouse (cracked panes, splintery
porch) outside Brattleboro.

Once town clerk, my steely grandma
squints behind smoky glass in the parlor.
Her mother's samplers sag in the upstairs hall.

The kitchen floor's the color of
store-bought cheese; the kitchen stove
has garlands of cast-iron daisies.

On an April Sunday I journey
over the fields, down to the murmuring swamp:
going to pick leeks and lilies, mint and chamomile.

Humming *"Rock of Ages,"* I inhale
the damp New England spring: America's
my dooryard, my quilt, my rag rug!

I've never eaten *potage parisienne,*
never drunk red wine,
never tasted olive oil,

but I've a skinny aunt beyond the hill
who makes Presbyterian love-drinks
from lilies and camomile and leeks!

Ginger Root

All week I've wanted to write a poem about the bin of ginger roots I pass in the supermarket—how each ginger root is a tiny rough-skinned ivory man, a tough homunculus twisted with the wisdom of the garden. But the poem falters, fades. . . . Pathetic fallacy! Untrue to ginger root!

Cabbages swell and fatten, voluble green heads confronting the sun like plain frank Texas girls, but ginger roots are like the inhabitants of some weighty inland sea, or like the seeds of a forest of Saturn, or like country children who have grown very old and witty at the center of the earth, so full of observation that every word they utter is passionate and keen, every sentence burns like Elizabethan verse. And then they lie quiet in the bin, asking with their silence: "What is the use of all this? Too little, too late?"

If every supermarket poet could go back into the valley of her past and lace it with ginger roots, what leafy poems might flourish then! What sestinas might be hot i' the mouth!

The Carrots

are clamped into black beds
like starfish tentacles, muscular fingers
the color of energy.

Some heat from beyond our constellations
got into them last summer
and made them thick and stubborn,

determined to get to the bottom of things.
When we try to dig them up they just
ignore us:

      we want their vitamin A
but they plan to eat our nitrogen
and they think they'll win.

Their fancy green plumes taunt us!
Like Amazon women disguised beneath
the feathery *chapeaux* of 1944,

they strut all night, plumes bobbing,
at the Copa—but every day at sunrise
it's back to the assembly line. . . .

Watch out for these secret agents!
Though they look frivolous, they're
single-minded:

                stuck in the mud like
a fleet of cast-off peg legs,
they give up the inessential

at the snap of a cap—the plumes,
the feathers, the Mr. John designs. . . .
When we lie down in the furrow

they'll turn all the iron of our bodies
into cold rust, cold
extragalactic sugar.

The Red Cabbages

stare like monster heads,
featureless beings,
each set regally in a tough
ruff as if to show
Shakespeare where to go.

An emissary from
here to there, a spy in
the vegetable kingdom,
I drift among them.
How did they come here,

what is their purpose, why
are their faces so
veiled, so flushed?
At the end of the garden
I meet a neighbor who tells me

"Frost last week! The turnips will be extra
sweet right now—"
but I hardly listen:
rustling through rows
of crimson I examine

leaf on leaf of silence, leaf on
leaf thick with the red
code of winter, each leaf
enclosing cold acrostics.
I'm sure there's a leathery hum, a slow

vibration rising
from every purple presence!
I believe they're humming to themselves,
humming and swelling, secret
agents of Arcturus!

And what are their stems accomplishing,
those trunks of ice, what
toes are they growing,
what joints and fingers?
Maybe I'll wait all night in the garden, maybe I'll let

the frost wind paint me white,
maybe at midnight
when the Dipper flashes overhead
and the moon sips the tide
the vegetable mysteries will be unveiled!

Storm clouds cross the sky, smoke signals:
the cabbages flicker their scarlet armour,
and I shiver, stuck up here
without a toe
in a single furrow.

Those aliens
play dumb as stones
but I know there's a firefly of syntax
gnawing at the silence
inside each red head.

Beets

You disguise yourselves as dark-skinned stones,
plumed in purple and green,
but perhaps you're really an army,
filing toward summer, crusaders
for sweetness and heat,
                              or perhaps
a caravan of Russian traders,
modestly shrunken but bearing
goods of great value—a cargo
of rubies, for instance,
and little magic sacks of blood. . . .

Dwarf heads, tiny warriors
rocking silently across the fields,
I know you know some secret!

Dry cold days when the ground is hard
you stick to your positions,
as if to say: *Context is all, order, origins.*
Pull me from my place in line
and I am lost!

But when the earth is wet and easy
you let go like drunken Cossacks,
as if murmuring, *Ah, pleasure*
of surrender, O happy nights
alone in the tavern, under the moon!

In long-ago Russia my twelve-year-old grandma,
the *shabbes-goy*, knelt in the black thick furrows
of the summer steppe, and plucked up
baskets and baskets of fat-cheeked beets.
Every night her peasant grandmother stewed them
and married them to sour cream, onions, cabbages.

When the long winter struck the tundra with iron,
they remembered that ritual meal, remembered—
as they sighed beside the great black Russian stove
and the samovar hissed and they scooped out
coals for the Jews next door—

that you were still marching somewhere,
that there was still a secret
procession of blood,
                              under the ground.

The Wild Grasses

the buckwheat, the thistle, the pointy-headed
dust-colored rushes seem to
float at the edge of the cliff
between me and the sea, a population
of millions, nodding, loving each other
like humble Galileans newly converted by
that rabbi in Jerusalem. . . .
                            Some underground
pattern threads them together,
some testament of roots,
as if their stems were strokes in a sentence
a buried prophet tried to write.

At twilight, when the salt cold breeze
sweeps over them, they're silent
as if in assent: they bow, they
flatten themselves at its feet.

I wonder what
nervous credo
knits them, succors them,
keeps them green
for so many weeks at a time.

Autumn Song

Twilight. Warm and moist.
The garden's dreary, desultory;
its green pushes at my eyelids
like a soft thick weight,
a green as sad as gray.

A few last summer squash poke out
gold thumbs, tired propositions;
tomatoes seal themselves in fine white
webs of frost and hang from stems
black as old scabs.

What is the strange ease in the furrows,
why do I want to lie down with the rotting
cabbages and heavy tomatoes
and wrap myself in a long voluptuous
sheaf of sleep?

The Celery Bushes

Almost October and the celery bushes have flowered
and now we know where the lost children went.
They went in among the green-white stalks,
the pale tall stalks that are cold and fluted
like the columns of the Parthenon,
and they were never seen again.
Except, on clear nights, when the moon is dark

and stars pierce the sky like needles,
the vigorous celery bushes faintly
rattle and hiss, their pillars sway apart,
their leaves curl and twist
as if in astonishment—
                      and very far away,
among the roots, we hear

the voices of the lost children.
One is down there hunting with silver arrows,
and one is climbing, hand over hand,
up the toughest thread of the tallest stalk.
When he reaches the top, he'll see the stars,
he'll yawn, he'll sing, he'll taste
the impossible celery flowers.

The Language of Flowers

1. Geranium

The tongue of the geranium is thick and pink.
At midday it breaks a fuzzy silence
to utter red letters
about the world beyond the pot:

an Alpine field where cows plod slow as boulders,
a thin fire in one corner
of the snowed-in barn
where Bavarian milkboys stand at dusk

singing, stamping, spreading their hands above the flame,
imagining geraniums in some
perfectly hot perfectly wordless
Italian noon.

2. *Impatiens*

tells itself rapidly and delicately
as a rosary in the hands of a decorous nun
who is secretly an unbeliever:

sentences of pallor, devouring
dark grounds around the roots,
moist clauses embracing each other

in their haste to come punctually
to a good green end
and a newer greener

beginning.

3. Lilies of the Nile

speak in blue voices
out of swaying necks,
a chorus of seeds and leaves.

In their sentences, slaves gather by the river
for a ceremony we've forgotten.
Sacred waters circle the roots,

the Dog Star burns overhead,
and the high stems of the lilies open
to speak Egyptian mysteries:

solemn and grand, their words sail toward us
like huge blue spores
or the silent feathers of cranes.

Each sigh inscribes itself in the air
with a cold stylus.
Somewhere inside each hieroglyph

we can see the face of the pharaoh
who decreed that line or phrase
seventy centuries ago.

4. Petunias

The extravagance of petunias!
White ruffs and baroque throats
of scarlet, orange, purple!
Each one conceited as a ceiling
the painter worked on for a year!

No hope of understanding that
rococo rhetoric, those wild
metaphors:
        Smiling and supple
the petunias bob, babble, jostle

till we can only guess
their meaning and admire
and say *Yes*.

5. *Bougainvillea*

writhes around the gate, all
sexy gasps, all
shivers of seduction.

When we say,
Be serious, explain yourself,
Sex isn't everything,

bougainvillea falls silent,
flutters in the heat,
lifts its silky petals to reveal

a syntax of scurrying blood cells,
a vocabulary of passionate
untranslatable colors.

6. Roses

utter the noblest syntax,
each blossom an archetypal crimson
noun,

each one the only one
of its kind,
as if Plato had breathed a few enormous

bubbles of color
and said, *Here you are, fellow philosophers,*
the dimensions of Dimension,

the language of absolutes,
and inside each rose a tiny glistening
god stood up

grasping a spear on which his own
particular rule of pollen
was darkly engraved.

7. Daisies

Common as prepositions,
speech of the ground,

daisies
link grass with tree,

seed with stone,
white with yellow

with green
with sun.

IX

From *In the Fourth World*
(1979)

Getting Fired, or "Not Being Retained"

A letter came in the mail from the Vice President of Crucial
    Events.

Though I tried not to open it, it got out of its envelope
like a secret agent who slips through a door when no one is
    looking.

The letter regarded me gravely and took stock of me as if it
    were
an uncle who had not seen me for twenty years.

Then it said: "Due to circumstances"—and something else I
    didn't hear—
"decisions have been made" it said "requiring that
and so in accordance with all established procedures you
are not being retained in your present position—that is—"
the letter took a quick puff of a cigarette
and grinned (an engaging grin, like the grin of a movie actor
who makes his fortune from his teeth and hair and lovable
    shoulders)—
"That is—" said the letter—"You're fired!"

"Awfully sorry to have to transmit this bad news"
the letter added, seeing my dismay,
"but that's how things are, you know."

I wasn't bothered. At least, I didn't think I was.
I went into the garden and sat down among
my old friends the rhododendrons and drank some coffee.
The rhododendrons held out five-fingered clusters like
new green stanzas they were writing—"What
do you think of this?"—and
I thought well of them and I was calm.

But in the meantime, while I wasn't looking, the letter
took possession of the house. The letter
stretched out on the living room sofa and asked for a newspaper,
which it scrutinized with eyes of steel.
"What's all this shit?" asked the letter sternly
when my children left their sweaters on the kitchen floor
or my husband played the phonograph too loud.

The letter unpacked its suitcases and hung up
an astonishing number of fancy jackets
(all dark tweeds, most
from Brooks Brothers and J. Press)
in my bedroom closet. The letter
sent people on errands and ordered special
delicacies from the supermarket—for its diet was
unusual: it liked the wings of new-hatched chickens,
the legs of live crabs, oysters white as
eyes, and carrots whose scream (when they
were ripped from the ground)
was recorded and verified by experts.

The letter took over my study and replaced all the books
with volumes from its own collection, all
black paperbacks, all untitled.

At last I couldn't stand
to be in the same house with the letter,
watching it raid the refrigerator,
seeing it read its black books,
and now I spend most of my time beneath the rhododendrons,
thinking careful thoughts—
"If first I—
then perhaps I—
after which, of course,
and so forth—"
while the letter scrapes carrots in the kitchen
for my children.

But the children,
bless them, have got used to the letter,
as though it really were a bad-tempered old uncle
with whom they have lived all their lives.

The Intruder

At first he's only a breath in the dark,
measuring himself out like a heartbeat,
discreet as the blood that flows and coils in places
we never bother to remember.
                              At first
he enters through cracks, in the light that leaks
unnoticed under the door from the bare hall
where the bulbs blister the nightlong fears of the children away,
in the damp that shreds the paper from the walls,
in the pane where the window refuses to hold itself together.

As first he's fast, coming and going
like something I thought I saw from the corner of my eye
but it was never there.
                        At first
he tells himself rapidly as a fairy tale
already told a hundred times.

But then we know he's here. Both of us know.
At once. You wake. You speak.
There's somebody here. A third breath.
We lie motionless in bed—what is there to do—
imagining and discarding the useless weapons,
that crystal lamp, the old mirror, the lightswitch,
the children, the children.

Someone has of course ripped out the phone.
We are all silent, together, in the dark.

The bed trembles. Yet still you do not move.
But I—at last I open my eyes.

And though

I do not see him (I see nothing)
at last his presence falls upon me, delicate and
tremendous as a shard of ice
falling into each eye.

The Giant Rat of Sumatra

"Matilda Briggs was not the name of a young woman, Watson,"
said Holmes in a reminiscent voice. "It was a ship which is associated
with the Giant Rat of Sumatra, a story for which the world is not yet
prepared."

—Sir Arthur Conan Doyle, "The Sussex Vampire"

Poor Watson, you never met him?
Befuddled in foggy London
you wandered the labyrinthine streets.
Down by the docks you found a violin

floating in murky waters,
waters blue-black and bruised by
too many nights. Later,
in your stuffy room,

you prescribed cocaine—
cocaine for the brain!—
but your prescriptions were intricate and
indecisive, like bad philosophy.

Days passed, days and days.
You were always lonely.
Medical metaphysician,
you could never figure anything out.

But Watson, dear Watson,
all the time, there he was!
There he still is!
The leaves part,

they're purple, they rustle.
The jungle moans with excitement.
The natives are restless tonight.
They have drums fiercer than violins,

their heads glisten like horsehair sofas,
heads on stakes.
Another hour and he'll come out.
Already the ceremonial fires are lit.

And Watson, he's so much bigger
than the ship *Matilda Briggs*.
His great fangs are taller than masts,
his tail is a sail heaving him along,

he walks like twenty-five earthquakes.
Sumatra bows before him.
Tomorrow he'll swallow the Thames,
he'll gobble Big Ben,

Westminster will cower,
Her Majesty will shudder,
and then—and then—
Ah Watson, don't you know him?

He's gray and massive like the fog.
His eyes gleam like copper kettles.
His ears are dark, so dark,
and his tongue so elementary.

Her Last Sickness

Sailing the long hot gulf
of her last sickness,
out past the whispering beach,
she saw the town lights dim.
What were those voices shouting in her head?
She was their sentence, they were hers.
Words ripped at her ribs
like multiplied hearts, until
she drowned in that intolerable pulse.

Now riding the slow tide
she's dumb as driftwood, sheds
her last light skins of thought
easily as October.
Mounting the great salt flow,
black with it, white with its foam,
she's picturesque—no more than a design
on the packed sand, hieroglyph
from another land.

After a Death

—for my father

I am far away from you.
In my front yard the uncontrollable rain
coats leaves and bark
with a medicinal, protective sheen.

What I inherit is impossible:
a car I can't drive,
empty coats in a closet,
a useless middle initial.

I am astonished by my calm.
Have you really left me no pain?
The enormous sky, floodlit by thunder,
recalls your cold home—

the comforting grass,
the black socket of stone
in which you are fixed
like a blind eye, directionless.

Mafioso

Frank Costello eating spaghetti in a cell at San Quentin,
Lucky Luciano mixing up a mess of bullets and
calling for parmesan cheese,
Al Capone baking a sawed-off shotgun into a
huge lasagna—
                    are you my uncles, my
only uncles?

        O Mafiosi,
bad uncles of the barren
cliffs of Sicily—was it only you
that they transported in barrels
like pure olive oil
across the Atlantic?

            Was it only you
who got out at Ellis Island with
black scarves on your heads and cheap cigars
and no English and a dozen children?

No carts were waiting, gallant with paint,
no little donkeys plumed like the dreams of peacocks.
Only the evil eyes of a thousand buildings
stared across at the echoing debarkation center,
making it seem so much smaller than a piazza,

only a half dozen Puritan millionaires stood on the wharf,
in the wind colder than the impossible snows of the Abruzzi,
ready with country clubs and dynamos

to grind the organs out of you.

Shell Collecting

At Black Point, collecting shells.
The sky smoke gray,
a few birds tossed in the wind—
dark motes, dark functions
of the eye.

Shells bloom in the tide pools.
Shells scuttle like spirits.
I imagine them clicking and speaking,
a poem of safety,
an epic of multiplicity.

On the cliff the raw grass
winds around itself,
tangling, untangling.
In the gray sea a thousand
storms are drowning.

Beside a cave at water's edge I find
an immense sea anemone,
almost invisible, packed in sand.
It quivers to the touch.
It is so naked I want to kill it.

Stirring still water with a stick,
I see, now, everywhere
anemones without shells
clinging to sand and rock,
silent, enigmatic,

and I long for the certainty of shells.
Can such nakedness be safe?
How should I live
when even the blackest rock
is elastic with life?

Grandmother

Each night I see myself in the white
mirror of sleep—

(is it myself
I see?)

—a face vast and wrinkled as the sea
at evening,

a vague face
withdrawing. . . .

Other faces, small and white and round as
peeled apples

fall from the long dark
face I wear:

my round grandchildren!
One is taking my nose away,

another my lips, a third my cheeks. . . .
In the morning

I find they've moved to California
with all my features intact

and only my eyes are left in
a face that is no longer mine.

The Dream of the Sun

Asleep on the beach, I step onto
the porch of the sun
where my father (seven years dead) sits in
a chair of scarlet wicker.
He smokes a cigar and looks at me calmly.

"I've been reading Nietzsche, Tom Paine, Guatama Buddha,"
he says. "I think I've found the answer."
"Daddy," I cry. "It's been so long!"
He motions to a yellow porch swing.
"Let's talk things over quietly, darling."

"I'm afraid." I tremble at the edge of the porch.
I cling to the railing. Below
black spaces swirl like the sea,
all round us an echoey roar as though
we had entered a giant shell.

"Daddy, I want to go back."
Sand flies tear at my flesh. I'm almost awake.
He throws away his cigar.
He rises sobbing. (He doesn't look well.)
"Sandra, Sandra, don't leave me here!"

The Cassandra Dream

I open my bureau drawer
and there I find
my beautiful cousin Cassandra.
She has a face like old linen,
yellow and soft,
dark hair that streams into the corners,
blank eyes like the eyes of a doll.
I realize she's waited for years in this drawer,
ever since my grandmother put her there.

I beg her to speak,
to tell me all she knows.
I invoke the tie of blood.
But it's no good:
she's motionless, mute, folded away like a sheet.
Only her cold hair, cold as a night river,
grows while I watch,
spills from the drawer,
swirls, tumbles,

drowns me in a dark prediction.

The Milk Dream

My breasts are full of milk.
They tower above me like peaked rocks
(though no one sucks).
Warily I touch the left nipple.
It's red as a strawberry, feels like rubber,
but rises from a white and stony
promontory.
This is the Not-Me
I think (calm, philosophical).
This hard white wall conceals some valley
tough with its own life.

Yet I long to enter,
to walk into the center of these mountains,
to find the little secret spring where warm milk wells,
not me, but mine.

I rise, I start on the journey.
I'm wearing boots, carrying a knapsack,
climbing, climbing.
The air is cold near the peaks.
There are few houses.
Already the sun has set
and blue winds flow by like tides.
Everywhere doors are closed,
windows made fast for the night.
All closed, all locked against me.

Lonely, I camp among the rocks
at the edge of my body.

The Dream of My Daughter

Officious, I begin
to brush my daughter's hair,
which is delicate and fair
as a green young fern.

She cries, she cries out
"Mommy, watch it,
I'm sensitive"—
but I'm unmoved, I'm passionate.

Like a large beaked bird
I tear, I tear,
I claw at her hair,
her hair green-golden,

her hair straw-light,
her hair of Rapunzel,
shredding, feathery,
descending around me,

her hair of pollen
which dissolves as I watch
to a thousand cells,
her hair of bees—buzzing, alive—

her hair of poison,
her hair of sun in the hive,
her hair that is melting like wax:
"Mommy, mommy," my daughter weeps,

but ruthless I rip it away—
"Rapunzel, Rapunzel, let down your hair"—
till the curls stream hollow and clear
like an empty river,

and only a few blonde burrs, a dying bush,
are left in the brush.

The Grandmother Dream

My Sicilian grandmother, whom I've never met,
my Sicilian grandmother, the midwife, who died
forty years ago, appears in my bedroom.
She's sitting on the edge of my bed,
at her feet a shabby black bag,
and she speaks a tangled river of Italian:
her Sicilian words flow out like dark fish, slippery and cold,
her words stare at me with blank eyes.

I see that she's young, younger than I am.
I see her black hair gleam like tar as
she draws from her small black midwife's bag
her midwife tools: heavy silver instruments
polished like doorknobs, polished—misshapen, peculiar—
like the knobs of an invisible door.

Doing Laundry

I am doing laundry in my laundry room
the washing machine grinds and pumps like my father's heart
it is sick   it is well
sick again   well again

behind the round window your shirts
leap and praise God slowly like gentle souls
and my old brassieres bound like the clean breasts
of antelopes

I am doing laundry in Africa
and overhead the parrots shriek
they encourage me to beat harder
beat the dirt out of the flowers

I am doing laundry in Indiana
my husband the insurance salesman comes in
wanting to know if I would like to buy his new
insurance against laundry

I am doing laundry in the river of Styx
I pound and I pound
the shirts disappear
the brassieres dissolve to nothingness

I am a heart doing laundry
and I beat and I pound
until I no longer remember
the color of dirt.

Tailors

—for Elliot

my grandfather the tailor sat in his little dark shop
sewing me together
(twice a day my Sicilian grandmother brought him
platefuls of praise like bowls of spaghetti)

my other grandmother the seamstress basted and hemmed
(her needle traced strange Russian characters
on the rough cloth)

your grandfather the tailor lengthened you
imperceptibly
(he lovingly made you a beard and a *tallis*)

and in the sultry sweatshops of the lower East Side
(where summer swelled like a giant cabbage)
hundreds and hundreds of great aunts
hunched over glittering machines
in the heavy weather
crooning and clucking and
weeping and gossiping

and stitching together the sidewalks
that would stitch us together

The Fireflies

Midnight. The fireflies
tighten their circle around the house.
The children are leaping away
like moths in the moonlight
while side by side in their heavy bedroom
man and wife, wife and man
slumber like trees,
twin trees with black bark. . . .

One A.M. The fireflies approach.
Points of cold heat, exclamations of light,
they stitch the darkness like Morse code.
Now they play among leaves,
now they puncture thick bark.
Pine needles hiss in the forest:
already the robins have flown
and the children vanished in moonlight whiter than cream.

Flashing, the fireflies draw nearer.
It is almost their hour.

In the Fourth World

in the fourth world
I grew wings and began to dance
in the fourth world
I started to write poems and couldn't stop
in the fourth world
my hair turned purple as the rings of Saturn
in the fourth world
I always knew who the murderer was
slept well woke early
didn't smoke
never ate too much
in the fourth world
my eyes were butterflies
opening
in the fourth world
someone I had never met before called me by my name
"come here a minute, Sandra"
and gave me a map on which was clearly marked
the way through suburbs airports deltas avenues
letters windmills tulips galaxies
to the fifth world
and the sixth world
and the seventh

Index of Titles and First Lines